# On Being

## in These Precarious Times

### CONTRIBUTORS

Carl E. Braaten
Stephan Turnbull
David S. Yeago
Nathan H. Yoder
James Arne Nestingen
Frank C. Senn
Sarah Hinlicky Wilson

Edited with an Introduction by
## Carl E. Braaten

Foreword by
## Bishop John F. Bradosky

Lectures Presented
at a Theological Conference
Sponsored by Lutheran CORE
and the
North American Lutheran Church

August 6-7, 2013

Sheraton Station Square Hotel
Pittsburgh, Pennsylvania

## ALPB Books
Delhi, New York

For a **FREE COPY** of
*Lutheran Forum* and *Forum Letter*
go online at: www.lutheranforum.org
and click on "Free Issue"

Cover photo:
Downtown skyline, Pittsburgh, Pennsylvania,
by Frederick J. Schumacher

The American Lutheran Publicity Bureau wishes
to acknowledge with deep appreciation the work of
William Fensterer in the proofreading of this text,
Dorothy A. Zelenko for assistance with photo artwork,
and Martin A. Christiansen for layout and design work.

Frederick J. Schumacher
Executive Director, ALPB

ISBN 1-892921-26-X

American Lutheran Publicity Bureau
PO Box 327
Delhi, NY 13753

*On Being the Church in These Precarious Times*
(Delhi, NY: ALPB Books, 2014), 136 pp.

# Contents

# Presenters

Rev. John F. Bradosky
   Bishop, North American Lutheran Church
   Columbus, Ohio

Rev. Dr. Carl E. Braaten
   Professor Emeritus of Systematic Theology
   at the Lutheran School of Theology at Chicago
   Sun City West, Arizona

Rev. Dr. James Arne Nestingen
   Professor Emeritus of Church History
   at Luther Seminary, St. Paul, Minnesota

Rev. Dr. Frank C. Senn
   Senior of the Society of the Holy Trinity
   Evanston, Illinois

Rev. Dr. Stephan Turnbull
   Senior Pastor of First Lutheran Church
   White Bear Lake, Minnesota

Rev. Dr. Sarah Hinlicky Wilson
   Editor of *Lutheran Forum* and
   Research Professor at the Institute for
   Ecumenical Research, Strasbourg, France

Dr. David S. Yeago
   Adjunct Professor of Lutheran Studies
   Gordon-Conwell Theological Seminary
   Charlotte, North Carolina

Rev. Dr. Nathan H. Yoder
   Pastor of St. Martin's Lutheran Church
   Maiden, North Carolina

# Foreword

## Bishop John F. Bradosky

It is an honor and a privilege for the North American Lutheran Church along with Lutheran Core to host this continuing series of theological conferences. It is a priority of the NALC to connect challenging theological presentations and dialog with the work of the church in conjunction with our convocation. These two will remain inextricably connected into our future.

We are truly grateful for the vision and extraordinary leadership of Rev. Dr. Carl Braaten and Dr. Robert Benne in selecting both appropriate themes and excellent theologians to guide our discussion. This year's theme, "On Being the Church in These Precarious Times" and the presenters whose work you are about to read are no exception.

These theologians remind us of the nature of the Church. "This is the assembly of all believers among whom the Gospel is preached in its purity and the holy sacraments are administered according to the Gospel" (Augsburg VII). Some of the presentations will explore Trinitarian theology, the specific work of the Holy Spirit, the office of the ministry, the sacraments, worship, oversight, church order, and a variety of other topics that are necessary for a meaningful discussion among those concerned with being the Church in light of the challenges we face. These are precarious times. According to Webster, "precarious" means: "depending on the will or pleasure of another; dependent on uncertain premises, insufficient foundation; depending on unknown conditions, uncertain developments characterized by a lack of security or stability that threatens with danger, peril, or great risk."

This is a time of growing uncertainty among Christians. Interest in denominational institutions is waning. Mainline denominations are in a state of statistical free-fall. Biblical illiteracy abounds. More Christians seem unsure of what it means to believe in Christ and live a Christian life. Fewer Christians seem interested in world mission. Many believe but few are equipped to share their faith with others. Even fewer seem concerned about the instability, danger and risk that are consequences of our struggle. Other forces seem stronger while the faithful either accept the presumed powerlessness of their context or resolve to join forces with those who presume to have power and use it. Could it be that both groups compromise the Christian faith in their struggle to cope with this context? One wallows in hopelessness and the other denies there is a problem.

There seem to be at least two forces at work making this a precarious time; popular pressure from the culture around us to conform and pressure from within the Church to preserve its organizations and institutions by adapting to cultural pressure, compromising for the sake of accommodating the values of those it hopes to incorporate into its life. This secularization is evident in the devaluing of the Scripture as one authority among many other authoritative books in the world. The secularized church no longer considers the Word "the norm" of its life and faith. Since there is no ultimate truth, relativism is not only acknowledged but embraced. In such a relativistic world it is impossible to make the assertion that Jesus is what he claims to be in Scripture, "I am the way, and the truth and the life; no one comes to the Father, but through Me" (John 14:6). His self-disclosure was affirmed by the Church in Acts 4:12: "And there is salvation in no one else; for there is no other name under heaven that has been given among men, by which we must be saved." Today those who preach and teach these things as literally true are considered divisive and marginalized, by many who claim to be Christian.

In the secularized church, mission work and evangelism are considered passé. The grace of Jesus Christ becomes the amorphous love of human invention requiring little or nothing from us except to tolerate, accept and include. In such a relativistic culture, sin for one is righteousness for another, so the less said about sin the more "loving" we seem. Moralism and political agendas become the "new gospel" proclaimed in liturgies and preaching, taught in Bible studies and Sunday School lessons. The new moralism is designed to subvert biblical morality and replace it with new understandings, including human sexuality, marriage and family.

These forces of secularization have kept many in the church acquiescent and silent. Other believers are content to become participants in the formation of a utopian world designed by philosophical and psychological principles that often have little in common with the Gospel of Jesus Christ. The proclamation of the Gospel of Jesus Christ, the kingdom of heaven he announced, his sovereign rule, a kingdom only realized through God's direct intervention in the life, death and resurrection of Jesus has been all but abandoned by many Christians. Instead they search for what the world will deem relevant to meet their needs and desires. Amid such futile attempts at relevancy and popularity the secularized church in North America becomes increasingly less effective in its ministry and less popular with those it seeks to please in the culture. These pressures from within and without diminish its redemptive capacity when the Gospel of Jesus Christ is not its clear and unequivocal proclamation. These divergent paths have resulted in the formation of new church bodies and painful separations in denominations in an attempt to bring clarity on what it means to be the Church as well as renewal and transformation to strengthen the church's capacity for mission and ministry in this culture.

The way forward in the midst of these precarious times is back to the Scripture and its authority, affirming the teachings of our confessional heritage. In his lectures on the Psalms Luther writes,

> What pasture is to the beast. . ., the nest for the birds, the stream for fish, the Scriptures are for believing souls. To the arrogant, of course, they are a stumbling block; he will have nothing to do with them, since they offer him nothing. But to him who approaches the Scriptures with humility they open themselves and themselves produce humility, change a man from a desperate sinner into a child of God. They give everything which the soul needs, and it is to tempt God, if anyone will not be satisfied with the Scriptures. They are the fountain from which one must dip. Each word of the same is a source which affords an inexhaustible abundance of water to everyone who thirsts after saving doctrine. God's will is completely contained therein, and we must constantly go back to them.

Regarding what it means to be the Church, Luther reminds us,

> It is not the Word of God because the Church says so, but because God's Word said so, therefore is the Church. The Church does not make the Word but is made by the Word.

In each of the presentations that follow, these theologians encourage a return to the Scripture, encouraging the faithful to read, study, meditate and be guided by the truth it holds. These presenters encourage us to consider and embrace again the foundations of our faith in our confessional heritage and the rich tradition of those faithful believers who preceded us and passed on the faith to us. Their witness reminds us that we are not the first Christians to face precarious times or great difficulties. The biblical and historical record of the Church is replete with examples of previous generations that endured such difficulties and responded with an even stronger and more passionate conviction in their proclamation of the Gospel of Jesus Christ.

We have great reason to be hopeful even in the midst of precarious times. There is good reason for us to remain silent no longer, to acquiesce no longer, but to cling to the hope we have in Christ and boldly proclaim the Gospel, following Christ as his disciples, committed to proclaiming it until the whole world knows, believes and becomes his disciples.

Without underestimating the serious issues that divide the Body of Christ in our quest to face these precarious times we must remember the first affirmation of Article VII in the Augsburg Confession. "It is also taught among us that one holy Christian church will be and remain forever."

We cannot destroy the Church. It will remain forever. As for the Word of God, according to Jesus, it will endure even after heaven and earth pass away. There is great consolation in the certainty of the Church and the Word. But there is also great responsibility for those who have been called, gathered, enlightened and sanctified by the one Holy Spirit, to remain in the one true faith in Jesus Christ, depending completely on that same Holy Spirit to believe in the promises that spring eternal from the Word, promises of forgiveness and eternal life.

It is my prayer as you read the work of these theologians you will find that hope, promise and encouragement for being the Church in these precarious times.

# The Church of the Triune God

## Carl E. Braaten

### Introduction

It is my distinct privilege to introduce the fourth annual theological conference sponsored by the Lutheran Coalition for Renewal and the North American Lutheran Church. The theme of this conference is: "On Being the Church in These Precarious Times." I will focus my reflections on two concerns: What kind of church are we talking about – there are churches and then there are churches – and what is so precarious about the times in which we live? When we survey the last two thousand years, many periods in church history were experienced as more precarious than ours. Think of the time of transition when the first followers of Jesus were all Jews to when Gentile converts were to be included. They had to rethink radically the laws of God's covenant with Israel having to do with circumcision, food and keeping the Sabbath holy. Thereafter came the Roman imperial persecutions, the barbarian invasions, the great schism between East and West, the Islamic invasions of North Africa and Europe, the post-Reformation wars of religion, the 20th century world wars between the so-called Christian nations of the West, and most recently the campaigns of the Nazis and the Communists to eliminate Christianity from the face of the earth. It would be wrong to claim that Christians and Churches in America today experience that kind and degree of suffering and martyrdom.

## The Secularization of Society and the Church

Our times are precarious in a different sense – in a more spiritual sense. "For we wrestle not against flesh and blood, but against principalities, against powers, against the rulers of the darkness of this world, against spiritual wickedness in high places" (Eph. 6: 12). Ever since the 18th century Enlightenment, Christianity in Europe and North America has had to contend increasingly with a militant secularization. By secularization we do not mean the separation of church and state. Rather, we mean the loss of religious substance in public culture, brought about by the drive to rid society of all religious symbols, ceremonies, and influence. We mean the massive prejudice against Christian beliefs and moral values within intellectual circles. Secularization includes the kind of practical atheism by which people live their daily lives as though there is no God. Secularization means the diminished respect for human life, both at the beginning and at the end of life, from the aborting of millions of the unborn to the euthanizing of helpless old people. Secularization means no moral boundaries, no normative frameworks, and no grand stories, such as the great biblical story of God reclaiming the whole of creation. Secularization means the dissolution of the idea of truth, the notion that everything is relative, that there's no right way to live or to think or to believe. It's all a matter of opinion, you know. I believe in Jesus; but that's just my personal preference. And whatever works for you is fine with me. I have a tennis friend in Arizona who is a Jew and an atheist. In his second marriage he married a pious Methodist woman who loves to go to church, which for him, he said, is all nonsense. But since it makes her feel happy, he's all for his wife going to church.

The secularization of society is one thing; the secularization of the church is something else. Secularization of

Christianity in Europe has reached an advanced stage. Church attendance is at an all-time low. Sundays are treated like any other days of the week. Traditional Christian beliefs are held rather loosely. More and more women are having babies without bothering to get married – and the same, of course, goes for men. Professor Douglas Farrow of McGill University has called attention to the effect of this phenomenon in Canada, in a book he entitled, *Nation of Bastards*. Both Protestant and Catholic Churches have undergone a massive defection from the practices and disciplines of the faith. The beautiful cathedrals in Europe are standing empty, kept open mostly as museums for tourists to recall the glories of ages past. What's happened to the churches in Europe is now befalling Christian institutions in North America.

How should churches respond to the dire demographic and sociological predictions? The worst possible way is to adapt to the secular standards in language, thought, and lifestyle. Many modern churches have adopted the strategy of blending into the surrounding culture. The strategy is well-intentioned. In order to not offend the cultural sensibilities of people whom we are trying to keep or convert, we tend to offer them religion in a secularist mode of pop culture, and to do whatever it takes to make the church seem relevant, familiar, progressive, entertaining, and downright chummy. Who wouldn't want to join a church like that? The more poignant question is: Who would? If the church cannot provide a message, a truth, a story, a hope that is totally other, not of this world, then why bother? Instead of acting like strangers and pilgrims whose citizenship is in heaven, we have become mere earthlings at home in our narcissistic, hedonistic, and materialistic society. Worship in the secularized church tends to become a quasi-entertaining spectacle that must "meet my needs," to provide me an emotional outlet, with laughter replacing reverence and silly stories a substitute for awe in the presence of the Holy One.

The church may very well have external enemies that wish to do it harm. It is important to identify such enemies and mount a smart counter-offensive, with the best apologetics that sanctified brains can muster. The enemies may be things like the Jesus Seminar, the New Atheism, Supreme Court Decisions, Gnostic spirituality, or whatever. But the more serious problem is this: the church is being undermined from within, tending to mimic the trends of the culture rather than embracing the testimonies and truths of the Bible. The Serpent of secularism plants the question, "Did God really say?" – then it follows with the false assurance – "You don't need to obey. You will not die!" The church is being subverted from within, by false prophets and fifth columnists, at times in the seats of leadership, theological and administrative. Will the church bodies be able to adjust in time before the spiral of decadence and death slowly but surely overtakes them?

Remember the story about the boiling frog? The story goes that if you drop a frog in boiling water, the frog will immediately jump out of it. But if you put the frog in a pan of water and raise the temperature slowly, the frog will stay where it is and eventually boil to death. Some churches are acting like the slowly boiling frog, gradually adapting – one assembly at a time – to the secular values surrounding them and enacting changes to conform to them.

It may very well be that churches that stand their ground will be pushed to the margins. So be it! There is no reason to feel so bad about that. We have been called to be faithful servants of the gospel, slaves of Christ, martyrs on a mission, not successful potentates of an imperial religion. Christianity began on the fringes of Graeco-Roman society. We are now being given by the providence of God a new opportunity for evangelization. A thoroughly secularized society gives rise to a sickness unto death that only the Christian faith can ultimately cure. The sickness is an existential sense of meaninglessness, ennui, boredom, and nausea, a profound sense of unhappiness and dissatisfaction. That's why ours is a society addicted to drugs. That's why there's an increasing rate of suicide among teens. The more secularization advances, the more it generates a need for something supremely other that can bestow meaning on human life. This meaning must come from a transcendent self-authenticating Divine Authority from beyond ourselves. We cannot give it to ourselves. We won't find it by dwelling within ourselves, by trying to pull it out of our guts.

## Retrieving the Great Tradition of Trinitarian Theology

But are we as a church ready to move into this vacuum? Armies understand that at times it's necessary to retreat before advancing. We will need to go back to the sources where it all began with Peter, Paul, and Mary and the rest of the apostles and evangelists, who bore witness to the God "who spoke to our ancestors in many and various ways, but in these last days he has spoken to us by a Son.... He is the reflection of God's glory and the exact imprint of God's very being" (Hebrews 1:1-3). What the church needs now is a retrieval of the Great Tradition of historic biblical and patristic Christianity. We are not calling for a boring repristination of a dead traditionalism. Remember the wise saying of Dr. Jaroslav Pelikan, of blessed memory: "Tradition is the living faith of the dead; traditionalism is the dead faith of the living."

I once heard an Orthodox Bishop explain the difference between dead traditionalism and living tradition. He told the story about an abbot with his monks meeting for evening prayer. The cat that lived in the monastery made such a racket that it distracted them. So the abbot ordered the cat to be tied up during the evening service. For years the cat continued to be tied up during evening prayer. And when the cat eventually died, another cat was brought to the monastery and tied up. Centuries later, learned theologians wrote scholarly treatises about *the religious significance of tying up a cat during evening prayer.* Dead traditionalism.

The only way to regain fidelity and jubilation in the modern church is to re-establish it on the foundations that have always sustained the one, holy, catholic and apostolic church of Jesus Christ. Churches that stray from their biblical, creedal, and liturgical foundations have fallen on hard times. They lose the will and the ability to teach the Catechism of the Christian faith and to pass it on to the next generation. Churches that leave their theology behind are soon left behind.

But there is some good news to report on the theological front. The most important theological event of the 20th century, in my view, was the revival of the classical Christian doctrine of the Trinity. We use the word "revival" because the doctrine of the Trinity all but died in the theological systems of 19th century liberal Protestantism. Immanuel Kant led the way by decreeing that "from the doctrine of the Trinity ... nothing whatsoever can be gained for all practical purposes."[1] None of the leading theologians of modern Protestantism – Friedrich Schleiermacher, Albrecht Ritschl, and Adolf von Harnack – had any use for the doctrine of the Trinity. For them it was an artificial construct – the amalgamation of Greek philosophy and Hebrew religion. The truth is that trinitarian theology taps into the deepest roots of the apostolic faith that virtually all Christian traditions officially claim to confess. This recovery of trinitarian faith is especially promising because of its broad ecumenical representation.

Starting with Karl Barth, a Swiss Protestant theologian, it was further advanced by Karl Rahner and Walter Kasper,

---

1. Jürgen Moltmann, *The Trinity and the Kingdom: The Doctrine of God*, trans. Margaret Kohl (Minneapolis: Fortress Press, 1993), p. 6.

Roman Catholic theologians. Two Lutherans, Wolfhart Pannenberg and Robert Jenson, made notable contributions to the recovery of trinitarian theology, as did Jürgen Moltmann, a Reformed theologian, as well as John Zizioulas, an Eastern Orthodox theologian, and Miroslav Volf, a Croatian coming from the Pentecostal tradition. The old denominational differences pale in theological significance compared to the great divide over the doctrine of the Trinity and the Christology on which it pivots.

I shudder when I hear preachers lament on Trinity Sunday that this is the occasion of the church year they dread the most. They've heard that the Trinity is a great mystery; they don't understand it. They can't figure out the arithmetic or how to unscramble the seeming contradiction that three can be one and one can be three. Is it like water that comes in three forms – liquid, ice, and vapor? Our good friend, Robert Jenson, addressed this theological conference three years ago on the doctrine of the Trinity. He published a little book that recorded conversations he had with his 8-year-old granddaughter, Solveig. Its title is *Conversations with Poppi about God*.[2] The outcome of the conversation was their mutual understanding that the Trinity is basically this: God the Father and his Son Jesus, the Man of Nazareth, and their shared Spirit as the power of the believing community, the church. The 8 year old granddaughter could understand that much, that the Trinity is the unity of the three whose names are God the Father, his Son Jesus, and the Holy Spirit shared by both of them. The Athanasian Creed says the same thing: The Father is not the Son, and the Son is not the Father, and the Spirit has his own personal identity, which is neither that of the Father nor of the Son. Theologians can make it more complicated than that, but that is the essential starting point for further reflection.

---

2. Robert W. Jenson and Solveig Lucia Gold, *Conversations with Poppi about God* (Grand Rapids, MI: Brazos Press, 2006).

If we understand the Trinity aright – how such a church doctrine came to be and what it says – we will get a lot of other things right as well. For one thing, we will be spared the kind of foolishness that appeared in the *Lutheran* magazine in May of this year, an article in which two Lutheran seminary professors aimed to teach the church about the Trinity. They twisted their explanations into some politically correct platitudes about gender. They warned that calling God the Father may promote male privilege and that, after all, there are many ways of speaking of the divine mystery, even in the Bible. The result is that no one learned what is important about the Trinity.

The doctrine of the Trinity does matter, because it alone provides the proper framework to answer the questions, "Who is Jesus?" And, "What is the Gospel?" And, "What is the Church in the world to do?" These are questions that our speakers will address at this conference. Jesus put this question to his disciples on the road to Caesarea Philippi: "Who do you say that I am?" The ancient church decided at the Council of Nicaea that it is impossible to answer that question properly apart from the doctrine of the Trinity. The Trinity requires a high Christology to make sense. A low Christology inevitably leads to some kind of unitarianism, in which Jesus is regarded as a prophet, to be sure, but not really God incarnate. Low Christology was already taught by some heretics in the ancient church, the Ebionites, the Adoptionists, and the Arians. In modern times low Christology is at home in liberal Protestantism. Schleiermacher, Ritschl, and von Harnack were its most famous 19th century theologians, the same trio that had no use for the Trinity. In present-day theology low Christology is what drives the beliefs of the radical feminist, process, and pluralistic theologians – a Sally McFague, a Schubert Ogden, and a John Hick. They still profess some kind of devotion to Jesus. They confess that Jesus is the focal point of their religious experience, even though they maintain we moderns can no longer consider Jesus the one true Savior of humanity. Supposedly, we moderns know now that all religions have their own savior figures and ways of salvation, and they are pretty much all equal. That puts an end to the apostolic mandate of world evangelization. Low Christology has won hands down in the religious studies' departments of universities and divinity schools, and even in mainstream church colleges and seminaries.

A high Christology starts with the fact that Jesus' naming of God his Father, his Abba, occurs no less than 170 times in the Four Gospels. In the Gospels "Father" is Jesus' name for the God of Israel; it is a name and not a mere metaphor or image. On account of Jesus' relation to his Abba and his promise to send the Holy Spirit, the early church gave a privileged status to the triune name of God as Father, Son, and Holy Spirit, although there are many other descriptors and metaphors for God in the Bible.

This triune naming of God would not have happened except for the resurrection of Jesus from the dead. A high Christology confesses that Jesus is the risen Lord, God the Son, sharing the glory of the Father. A high Christology is anchored in the Easter witness of the women and the disciples who attested, "He is not dead but alive; we have seen him, even his wounds." On account of faith in the living Jesus and inspired by the Spirit of Pentecost, the apostles and the early Christians began to speak of Jesus and God in the same breath. The Nicene Creed says it succinctly: Jesus Christ is "true God from true God, begotten not made, of one being with the Father."

So what does the Trinity have to do with being the church in these precarious times? Absolutely everything, my friends! The trinitarian paradigm frames the church's understanding and proclamation of the gospel of Jesus Christ. Ecumenically speaking, we do not wish to cooperate in joint witness and worship with those who trumpet a different gospel. That sounds harsh and narrow minded in an ecumenical age. But we must not forget that the apostle Paul admonished the Galatian Christians who were turning to a different gospel that "if anyone proclaims to you a gospel contrary to what you received, let that one be accursed" (Gal. 1: 8). Let that one be damned. The Trinity doctrine tells every generation of Christians which gospel they are to believe, teach, and confess. The Athanasian Creed put the matter quite strongly: "Whoever wants to be saved should think thus about the Trinity." It is necessary for the church even today to teach the doctrine of the Trinity to tell the difference between the truth of the gospel and all its fashionable rivals within and outside the churches.

## The Trinity, Church Unity and Mission

The Trinity is for us a model for thinking about the unity of the church. It offers us a starting point for thinking of church unity as a communion of believers and assemblies founded on the gospel of Jesus Christ. The unity of the church is based on the Trinity. According to Ephesians 4: 4-6, "There is one body and one Spirit ... one Lord, one faith, one baptism, one God and Father of us all." St. Cyprian stated that the church is "a people brought into unity from the unity of the Father, the Son and the Holy Spirit."[3] In the Trinity we do not find a static unity but a one-ness in three-ness, a unity which gives value to relationship, reciprocity, and mutuality between members of a loving communion of equals.

The unity of the church is for the sake of God's mission. Jesus prayed "that all may be one, so that the world might believe" (John 17: 21). The church understands itself to be a people elected to serve the triune God for the benefit

---

3. Walter Kasper, *The God of Jesus Christ*, trans. Matthew J. O'Connell (New York: Crossroad, 1984), p. 247.

of all peoples and nations. The mission of our church is the mission of the triune God. The church does not move God around the world on boats and airplanes. God moves the church around the world through the ongoing activities of all three persons of the Trinity. The sending of the church to the world is a continuation of the Father's sending of the Son and the Spirit. These sending operations aim to awaken faith and to start new communities of believers and disciples. The Holy Spirit leads the church to open new fields of mission and to continue the apostolic history that began at Pentecost in Jerusalem. As Robert Jenson says so aptly: "the first gatherings of believers were gatherings of missionaries."[4] This is our identity as the church of the triune God. If we surrender this missionary identity – as most of the mainline Protestant churches have done to a great extent, all the while talking a lot about mission such that everything becomes mission, even the pension fund – I repeat, if we surrender this missionary identity given by the triune God, we will be doomed to serve other gods, perhaps the neo-pagan gods of race, or nation, or class, or culture.

Should the church today continue to evangelize the nations in the name of the triune God? The answer is clear. The church is constituted by the structure of the trinitarian mission of God in the history of salvation. The church is the creation of God's Word to reach the world with the gospel of the triune God. Each person integrated into the Christian community is baptized into the triune name. Each person is nourished at the Lord's Table, whose eucharistic liturgy is intertwined with the trinitarian name of God. The Father is praised, the Son is remembered, and the Spirit is invoked.

A church that gathers all its members around the Word and the Sacraments should not be confused about whether

---

4. Robert W. Jenson, *The Triune Identity* (Minneapolis: Fortress Press, 1982), p. 29.

the Lord's commission to evangelize the nations is still valid. Any church that neglects the Great Commission has entered into a state of self-contradiction, or worse, betrayal of its Lord's command "to go and tell the gospel to all the nations." The church's call to mission is a matter of life and death. To question the permanent validity of the church's call to mission is to tear it out of its proper trinitarian and Christological framework. The church's mission to all the nations is a participation in the works of the triune God.

The Trinity is the basis and motivation for ecumenism and mission. While its center is in Christ, its circumference is as wide as the whole of creation. The Trinity provides the church with the most comprehensive framework for envisioning its place in world history, to interpret rightly the forces of secularization, science, and technology, to motivate care for the earth and its fruits, to stimulate dialogue between the religions, yes, but never to surrender the uniquely salvific meaning of Christ, and to promote international trends toward a peaceful world that will augment justice and freedom for all, without becoming sycophants of any ideology, whether of the left or the right. This means that the mission of the church includes concern for what Lutheran theology places under the kingdom ruled by the left hand of God – taking responsibility for all the conditions under which people live their daily lives. To be sure, the church's primary mission is to spread the gospel of Jesus to the ends of the earth until the end of time. This action is directed by the right hand of God. But the God of the Bible is ambidextrous. By his left hand he governs as providential Lord of the universe. It is necessary to distinguish but never separate the works of the two hands of God that define the two dimensions of the church's holistic mission. Together they have to do with the quality of life within this world as well as the promise of hope for an everlasting future beyond the here and now. Within a trinitarian vision of reality the church understands itself to be driven by the Spirit in every direction and into every dimension of life, never forgetting, however, that its center and criterion are given in the gospel of Jesus Christ.

It is within and by the church that we come to know the triune God, and in knowing the triune God we are given a true understanding of who we are as the body of Christ, the communion of redeemed sinners. By the indwelling grace of the Holy Spirit the church is created to be an image of life in communion with the three persons of the Holy Trinity. The speakers at this conference will address various aspects of the nature and purpose of the church, its structure and attributes, promises and problems. The series of presentations will begin where the church began, with the outpouring of the Holy Spirit as recorded in the Book of Acts. Without the creative work of the Holy Spirit we would have no connection with the mystery of salvation in the Word of God made flesh. Without the Spirit, the Bible is just a book of ancient texts and not the Word of God. Without the Spirit creating faith, the gospel would be and is dismissed by many as a myth. Without the Spirit the church is merely an association of like-minded people who gather for good fellowship and potluck suppers. Without the Spirit the sacraments are mere aids to remember events in the life of Jesus.

The speakers at this conference will lead us more deeply into the matters I have introduced in these opening remarks.

# Holy Spirit, Creator of the Church

**Stephan Turnbull**

It feels more than a little strange to me to be making this presentation in Pittsburgh. You see, I have a complicated relationship with the city of Pittsburgh. I am from Cleveland, Ohio, which means that I grew up rooting for the Cleveland Browns. And I don't want to exaggerate, so I'll just say that as I grew up in Cleveland we thought of the Pittsburgh Steelers as something like the manifestation of pure evil. Eventually, though Cleveland lost the Browns and we realized that real evil resided in Baltimore, which was surprising since Baltimore had once lost the Colts and we all thought of them as innocent. Who knew? And during the years that Cleveland had no football team, there was a strange kind of bond that formed between Cleveland fans and Pittsburgh fans. There was a shared understanding that things like this shouldn't happen in a benevolent universe, and that now we can both hate Baltimore. But then we got the Browns back, and I'm pretty sure everybody hates each other again now, just the way God intended. So I guess everything's back to normal, and everybody knows their role again, except for me. I never moved back to Cleveland, and I never got to bond with the new Browns. So I'm still stuck in this complicated place. I've been in Pittsburgh for the last 3 days and have discovered that it's really a wonderful place, and I am truly glad and honored to be here with you today.

All this talk about complicated loyalties and conflicted relationships leads me to my topic for today: the church. Or, more specifically, the Holy Spirit and the creation of the church. I think we should admit that we have some complicated church relationships among us. There are different Lutheran denominations and brands among us, which is already in some ways a plague upon all our houses, even as it simultaneously provides the opportunity for shoots of new growth in the burned over ground. I think we find ourselves in a period of pretty significant spiritual discernment. We are trying to discern what God is doing in our little segment of his church. What is God calling into being here and now that previously was not?

And so with my assigned topic for today, Holy Spirit: Creator of the Church, I hope to take us back to some theological foundations, some biblical and theological convictions to ground our discerning as we grope our way forward. In particular I'd like to build a three-legged stool here. I think if we can get our heads and hearts around these three things, it will give us a steady platform to think from and some strength to stand on.

## Spiritual Victory

The first leg of this metaphorical stool is spiritual victory. As the Holy Spirit creates the church, the church becomes a part of the spiritual victory of God. I recognize that a phrase like "spiritual victory" will strike some ears as un-Lutheran somehow. If that is the case, I simply ask that you would give me the benefit of the doubt for a moment. I need to explain what I mean by that.

Perhaps some of you will remember the Tom Hanks move *Castaway*. The movie came out in the year 2000, and in it Tom Hanks' character is stranded on a Pacific island after a plane crash. There's a famous scene in which this character finally succeeds in creating fire and then dances and celebrates around his fire with pride and joy. At the climax of his victorious celebration he spreads his arms and shouts for the empty island to hear, "I have made fire. I, I have made fire!" I share this with you to set up a reading of Ephesians 3, a passage that paints a picture of God's victorious proclamation of his defeat of the spiritual forces of evil in creating the church and lighting the fire of his Spirit in us.

There's a tense build up that begins in 3:2, with Paul practically teasing the Ephesians. "Surely you've heard of the administration of God's grace that was given to me...the mystery made known by revelation...so you'll be able to understand my insight into the mystery of Christ...nobody knew about it until it was finally revealed...." One imagines the Ephesians screaming, "Enough, tell us already!" Then he reveals the mystery: "This mystery is that through the Gospel the Gentiles are heirs together with Israel...." Here among 21st century hearers, I can almost hear the yawns in response. "Really, that's it? That's the mystery? The Gentiles get to be in too? Big Deal!" But if we are disappointed in this revelation, it only further reveals how far we have fallen from Paul's evangelical vision, how prone we are to separate the spiritual victory of God from the material realities of his creation.

Paul says that he became of a servant of this Gospel that unites all people in God's people through Jesus Christ, and this grace was given to him: "to preach to the Gentiles the boundless riches of Christ and to make plain to everyone the administration of this mystery." The first half of this grace is his kerygmatic calling. He was conscripted for the joy of telling people about Jesus who did not know about Jesus yet. We have precious little record of this joyful activity, his first-hand proclamation of the Gospel in scattered Mediterranean towns and synagogues. And perhaps our lack of records contributes to our lack of sharing in this evangelical task. God grant that we would do more of it, that our churches would be used by the Holy Spirit to extend the creation of the church in all the places we live and gather. The second half of this grace is Paul's theological calling, his systematic and didactic task. This is the *raison d'être* for much of his epistolary work and, in my view, also partly responsible for his various visits to Jerusalem to give an account of his work in the diaspora. This is the task we share here in this conference. We are explaining the administration of the mystery of the Gospel from and for a variety of perspectives.

Then comes the climactic verse of this ecclesiological explanation: "His (God's) intent was that now, through the church, the manifold wisdom of God would be made known to the rulers and authorities in the heavenly realms, according to his eternal purpose that he accomplished in Christ Jesus our Lord." Were you a little underwhelmed when you heard that church unity was the mystery of the Gospel? (Perhaps I should note here that ecumenism may or may not coincide with genuine unity. We live in an age of terrible denominationalism, and much of our life is symptomatic of that particular facet of our fallenness. But rearranging the bureaucracies of fallenness does not redemption make.) Then listen to Paul. The overcoming of the fundamental human reality of dividedness with the even more fundamental creational reality of human peace is part and parcel of the victory of God over sin. Sin divided humans from God. Sin divided men and women. Sin divided human beings from one another. Sin drove us from the Garden to the Tower of Babel. But the Holy Spirit of God, through the declaration of the Gospel, has created the church. It is the new creation of human community, in the new Adam Jesus Christ, the purpose of which is to be held up by God in the face of the spiritual forces of evil and to say: Ha! I win. I am God alone as I always have been. Where were you when I laid the foundations of the world and when I dug the fountains of the deep? Where were you when I stretched the stars in the sky? And where are you when I join together what you have rent asunder. Behold, look what I have done. I have made the church! I, I have made the church. It is fire; it will burn with my own presence; and it will burn brightly as the light of the world. His intent was that now, through the church, the manifold wisdom of God should be made known to the rulers and authorities in the heavenly realms.

I am no longer underwhelmed by this. But I am certainly disabused of my triumphalism. It hardly needs to be said that we are not fully living into this biblical vision. We dare not be triumphalist, but God's triumph is undiminished. The Holy Spirit is the creator of the church and the church is a manifestation of God's spiritual victory in Christ.

## Eschatological Hope

The second leg of the stool is eschatological hope. As the Holy Spirit creates the church, we experience eschatological hope. The presence of the Spirit in the church is a sign of the fulfillment of God's plans in ages past. And it is also a sign that God's fulfillment is not yet fulfilled.

A word picture from Paul illustrates this point well. It is a picture that appears in Ephesians 1:14 and 2 Corinthians 1:22 and 5:5. All three passages use the image in similar ways, and I'll use 2 Corinthians 5:5 simply as one example. "Now the one who has fashioned us for this very purpose (our eternal redemption) is God, who has given us the Spirit as a deposit, guaranteeing what is to come." The word in question is the one translated here as "deposit." In Greek it is *arrabon*. The term is also translated by others as "down payment," "pledge," "guarantee," or even "earnest money."

My wife and I bought our first house about a year after we were married. It was located on Daniels Farm Road in Mebane, North Carolina. Technically it was in Cheeks Township, but we didn't like to say we lived in Cheeks. Though I like to point out that, being in the northern part of the township, we definitely resided in Upper Cheeks and not Lower Cheeks. This was our first house and we experienced the joys of being first time home owners, which included the challenges that go with it, including the squirrel which one night swam up out of our toilet. That's a moment we'll never forget. But it was a sweet time of life. And I remember when we signed the contract and paid the earnest money. We were excited. We began planning and preparing and getting ready to move. That particular phase of the purchase and that particular phase of life were gifts to both us and the people selling the house. Those were good times. But it was also no substitute at all for actually closing the sale and moving in to the promised piece of land. The night we moved in we sat down on the front porch and took up residence in a land flowing with milk and honey – which for us meant that we ate a bucket of Bojangles fried chicken and drank 2 liters of strawberry soda out of the bottle. Sweet salvation. But first came the earnest money. The deposit of that check signaled a new and different moment in our lives. The plans of our past had reached their fulfillment. Only that fulfillment wasn't quite fulfilled yet. Paul says that the Holy Spirit is given to the church, to the community of Jesus, as earnest money or a deposit of the full inheritance which is to come.

But this isn't just Paul. The church is also pictured as a sign of eschatological fulfillment in the great story of the church's birth on Pentecost. Jews from all over the world were gathered in Jerusalem for the Pentecost holiday. Not coincidentally, this is the festival of first fruits, signifying the full harvest to come. While they were gathered, they heard the sound of a mighty rushing wind, and they saw something that looked like tongues of fire sitting on top of one another's head, almost as if Tom Hanks himself had been there. And the Holy Spirit filled the disciples of Jesus who were there and caused them to speak in other languages. This caused quite a bit of concern. Some people thought they were drunk.

Peter says there's no way they're drunk. It's only 9 in the morning. It's not wine; it's the Holy Spirit. And this outpouring of the Holy Spirit is the fulfillment of eschatological prophecy. Peter quotes from the prophet Joel to explain their experience, "In the last days, declares the Lord, I will pour out my spirit on all people. Your sons and daughters will prophesy, your young men will see visions, your old men will dream dreams. Even on my servants, both men and women, I will pour out my Spirit in those days, and they will prophesy." Peter quoted from Joel 2, but he could also have quoted from other Old Testament prophets such as Isaiah, Jeremiah, or Ezekiel who also prophesied the outpouring of the Spirit of God as a feature of the age to come. This is a sign of eschatological hope.

This eschatological presence of the Spirit in the church complements the spiritual victory of God in the church to pervade the whole creation in all of its dimensions. Previously in Ephesians 3 we saw that a divinely empowered human reconciliation was a sign of the victory of God in Jesus Christ to the inhabitants of the spiritual realm. Now in Acts a divinely empowered outpouring of the Spirit is a sign of God's victory in Christ to the inhabitants of the human realm. From both perspectives, God is defeating the power of Sin and Death and filling us with hope in Christ.

## Christ the Center

The third and final leg of the stool is the recognition that, as the Holy Spirit creates the church, Christ is the center of that creation. This leg is not equal to the other legs. This final leg is the leg that gives meaning to the others. The spiritual victory that God wins in the church, he wins through the cross of Christ. The eschatological fulfillment that God accomplishes in the church he accomplishes in the coming and second coming of Jesus. Christ is the cornerstone, without which everything else falls down. As I have told my church family back in Minnesota, if we could ever take the name and story of Jesus out of whatever we're doing and still have it function just fine without him, then we're doing it wrong. And if we don't change it, we can change the sign out front to say First Lutheran Supper Club and sell it to someone else, because we won't be the church anymore. Christ is the center of the Holy Spirit's creation of the church. Let me give you three little snapshots of this in the New Testament.

The story we just read in Acts 2 is generally regarded as the story of the birth of the church, though one could argue that it was already conceived and nurtured before this. But now it finally breaks forth into the world. The Spirit is poured out on the church, and it is released into life. What is too rarely noticed, I think, is the parallel that Luke has drawn between the birth of the church in Acts 1-2 and the birth of Jesus in Luke 1-2. Both are conceived by the descent of the Holy Spirit, after the announcement of an angel, and incarnated in human flesh. Both are sent out into the world in a humility only God could have imagined. The Gospel of Luke is the biography of the incarnate Christ in the person of Jesus of Nazareth. The book of Acts is the biography of the Spirit of the ascended Christ incarnated in the church. In the Gospel of Luke, Jesus came announcing that the Kingdom of God was at hand. In the book of Acts, his Spirit leads the church to announce that God has seated Jesus at his right hand to reign as the world's true Lord and King. Christ is at the center of who we are, or we are not the church.

These parallels in Luke's two-volume masterpiece also suggest that we should not under-read Paul's Body of Christ metaphor for the church. In fact, and here I realize full well that I am running beyond what any of us can reasonably hope to know, one wonders what kind of conversations Luke and Paul had while they were on the road together, maybe sitting by a fireside in Philippi, that lead these two fertile and spiritually inspired minds to teach us about Jesus and his church. When we read Paul's Body of Christ metaphor, I think we usually see it as nothing more than a convenient way of illustrating the needed lesson that we all have our own roles to play. As a body has eyes, ears, hands, and feet, so the Body of Christ needs apostles, prophets, evangelists, and teachers. And certainly Paul does mean that on any reasonable reading of 1 Corinthians 12. But this language is more powerful than a simple description of functional diversity or mutual interdependence. Christ already had a body. He was born with it, grew up with it, used its mouth to teach, and its hands to touch. Its face was set for Jerusalem, and its side was eventually pierced on a Roman cross. It was buried in the earth, and on the third day it was raised again from the dead and ascended to sit at the right hand of the Father. Christ was not without a body. And yet Paul says, "You are the Body of Christ." This is not a truth to be trifled with. Christ is at the center of who we are, or we are not the church.

Finally, last snapshot, I believe we can see this conviction leaking out into the Bible's other, passing descriptions of those of us who are the church. Do you know, for example, what term Paul uses most often to describe Christian people? It's not "Christians" of course. That hardly ever appears in the Bible, though that term does also ground our identity in Christ. It's also not believers or saints. In the undisputed letters of Paul we are called believers 23 times and saints 42 times. That's probably worthy of its own study. But in those same letters we are called brother or sister 127 times. The letters of Paul designate us as brothers and sisters in Christ far more than they identify us by any other term. And we are brothers and sisters *in* Christ because we are first of all brothers and sisters *of* Christ through faith. We are brothers and sisters of the first born and only begotten Son of

God, and *because of him* we are children of God. Romans 8 says that Jesus is the first born among many brothers and sisters, and that it is our destiny in the Spirit to be conformed to the image of the Son. It is our destiny and the work of the Spirit to have the created image of God restored in us as Christ is formed in us. Christ is at the center of who we are, or we are not the church.

The Holy Spirit is the creator of the church. And as we discern our way forward as the church, we will do well to build on at least these legs of the stool: Spiritual Victory, Eschatological Hope, and Christ at the Center of it all.

Now, if you will permit me, I would like to finish in a little different gear. You see, I am delighted to be here. I love being with you and sharing a passion for biblical theology with you. I think it is terribly important for the church to do this, to ground ourselves deeply and reflectively in the story of God. And thanks are due to the leadership of Lutheran CORE and the NALC for their commitment to these events.

But it will kill me if we leave this here. It will break my heart and waste all of our time if we come here and think godly thoughts and fail to respond in the church the Holy Spirit is creating out there, in all the places where we live, serve, and worship. And so I want to conclude by appealing to you to join in with the work of the Spirit as he creates the church in your world. Just as the Spirit hovered over the waters at the beginning and called into being that which previously was not, so I believe the Spirit is actively creating the church out of you and me and millions of people who don't even know Jesus yet. And somehow in the unfathomable wisdom of God, he uses you and me to tell them about him. To borrow again the language of Ephesians 3 with which we started this session, we gather in places like this for the sake of our theological task, to make plain the administration of this mystery, but we are sent out there for evangelism. We are sent out there to declare to the Gentiles the boundless riches of Christ.

And this is fun in here. But we do this for that. And that is sheer joy. It is unmitigated, unbridled, rapturous joy to actually share the good news of Jesus with others, to see people discover the love of God in Christ and to walk with people into newfound freedom and holiness. Every August in our church we gather at the lake to celebrate a group of adult and teen baptisms, in addition to the many infants we baptize all year long. We're going to do this in a couple weeks, and I am giddy with expectation. I can't wait. It's one of the high points of my year every year. And I brought along a short video of last year's baptisms so that I could share with you one tiny visual example of the Holy Spirit creating the church. And I know you don't know the people in the pictures, so this will probably be more indulgent for me than for you, but I hope you'll be able to see the joy in their faces nevertheless. I hope you will see the joy of knowing God in Christ and experiencing the wash of his forgiveness and the entrance into a new life and the welcome into his family. I hope you will see the Spirit of God hovering over the waters again, and I hope you will hear his invitation to join in the creative work, to make disciples of all nations.

*[This presentation concluded with a short video of a group of baptisms and re-affirmations of baptism to help us celebrate the gift of new life and new birth into the family of God.]*

# Word, Church, and World

## Lessons from the
## Theological Declaration of Barmen

## David S. Yeago

The Church is under pressure. The leading lights of culture and the academy have long since abandoned the Christian view of the world; many regard it as harmful and primitive superstition. The surrounding middle-class culture no longer upholds the church in its attempt to pass on the faith to new generations. Fundamental human institutions are being redefined, culturally and even legally. The government is engaged in a project of social reconstruction, and expects the whole of society, including the church, to fall in line with its vision of justice. It has come to the point that churches are being pressured by the state to do things contrary to their traditional morality, but demanded by the new morality of those in power. Many of the churches' leaders and pastors are fully on board with these developments; others are confused or demoralized. Mainline churches have little recent history of resistance to the dominant culture; to many, the very idea seems somehow extreme or disreputable.

That may sound like a description of the present situation of the churches in North America – the end of even nominally Christian culture, which has now spread far beyond the intellectual and artistic elites into the depths of popular culture; the breakdown of catechesis and Christian formation in mainline churches; the redefinition of marriage; the new kind of political pressure on the churches represented by the Health and Human Services mandate. But at a formal level, the description could just as well apply to the German Churches in 1933 – widespread de-Christianization, redefinition of institutions basic to our humanity, new moralities, an ideologically-committed state bringing pressure on the church to fall in line.

Now, I realize that playing the so-called "Nazi card" is considered very bad form indeed these days, and I am by no means accusing contemporary post-Christian elites in or out of government of being Nazis. The peculiar evil of Nazism is not, thank God, on our horizon, though it should perhaps give us pause that easy destruction of unborn life is widely touted as central to the *social justice* of our post-Christian order. What we do have that is similar are mainline churches whose cultural and political environment has changed drastically, churches faced with fundamental questions about their own mission and relationship to the world, churches which are deeply uncertain about just those matters.

Eighty years ago next May, a group of Lutheran, Reformed, and Prussian Union pastors and theologians gathered in the Berlin suburb of Barmen to consider such issues, under far more threatening circumstances than those we face today. The "Theological Declaration" which they produced is one of the great documents of twentieth-century church history; it has been a persistent, unsettling presence in theology and church for eight decades. Right or wrong, adequate or inadequate, it cannot be denied that the Barmen Declaration addresses the very issues that face our churches today, and does so at the level of deep theological principle. To mark the coming eightieth anniversary, to give focus to my presentation, and generally because I object to reinventing the wheel, I shall address my topic today by commenting briefly and selectively on the six articles of the Theological Declaration of Barmen.

Before going on, however, some words of caution need to be said. After World War II, as the full extent of the horror became known, Christians all over the world were in desperate need of heroes, symbols of Christian response and resistance. For Protestants, the Confessing Church was the obvious place to look, and Dietrich Bonhoeffer was its most visible figure. This led to what we might call a "heroic" interpretation of the German Church Struggle: the Confessing Church as a gallant resistance movement to the Nazis, with the Barmen Declaration as its banner.

Subsequently, historians began looking at the Church Struggle with a cooler eye, and there emerged what might be called a debunking interpretation. It's true: the Confessing Church never in fact repudiated the Hitler regime as such, it numbered supporters of National Socialism in its ranks, and it was very nervous about making statements that touched on public life. Most disturbing of all, the Confessing Church never spoke out on behalf of the Jewish people. In that light, its response to the Nazi revolution can be seen as rather insular and "churchy," missing the moral and political big picture.

Spiritually and theologically there was more to Barmen and the Confessing Church than the debunkers can see, but I do believe that it is critically important for us to avoid the heroic interpretation. That approach allows us to let ourselves off the hook much too easily: "If the German Protestant churches in the 1930s produced a heroic resistance to evil, well, then, doubtless we would too." We Lutherans in particular have too often clothed ourselves in Dietrich Bonhoeffer's righteousness and failed to realize how isolated he was in German Lutheranism and even in the Confessing Church. We have assumed that he *represents* us when in fact he is more truly a *judgment* on us.[1]

The Barmen Declaration was at best a *minimal* starting-point that ought to have led to repentance and conversion

1. On all such matters, see now the remarkable book of Paul R. Hinlicky, *Before Auschwitz: What Christian Theology Must Learn from the Rise of Nazism* (Eugene, OR: Cascade Books, 2013).

on a larger scale. For some communities and for some individuals it played that role, but by and large German Protestants, German *Lutherans*, missed the boat. The Confessing Church never matured corporately in its repentance and conversion to the point of responding in an adequate way to the great moral crisis of the 1930s and 1940s.

Yet if the Barmen Declaration is only a beginning, still, starting-points are not to be despised. The first step in climbing out of a pit is taking hold of the rope. My hope for this lecture is that with the help of the Declaration we may at least get our hands on theological truth that will support us in our own repentance and conversion, and in our own efforts to learn what it means to be the church in this place and time.

## ARTICLE I

It is central to any Reformation account of the church that the church is, as Luther put it, *creatura verbi*, the creation of the Word. The church exists because its members have been called and brought together by a message, a message that comes from God; the church only lives and flourishes as it persists in hearing that message and testifying to it. The Barmen Declaration goes to the heart of the matter in its very first article:

> Jesus Christ, as he is attested to us in Holy Scripture, is the one Word of God, which we have to hear, whom we have to trust and obey in life and in death.
>
> We condemn the false doctrine that the church can and must acknowledge as source of its proclamation other events and powers, figures and truths, as the revelation of God, other than and alongside of this one Word of God.[2]

---

2. Translations of the Barmen Declaration are my own from the text online at: http://www.ekd.de/glauben/bekenntnisse/barmer_theologische _erklaerung.html. A complete translation may be found in the appendix to this essay.

There is a theological controversy about this article which needs to be addressed. Some Lutherans, in the 1930's and still today, have rejected this article on the grounds that for Lutherans the church must proclaim *two* words of God, the law and the gospel. The issue is exacerbated by the fact that the drafter of this article was the great Reformed theologian Karl Barth, who had notable disagreements with Lutherans about law and gospel.

My own view is that this objection is misplaced. The context in which this article should be read is not the debate between Barth and Lutheran theologians, but the struggle of the Barmen confessors to resist the pressure of Nazi ideology and the seduction of Nazified theologies. The question here is, "By what Word is the church gathered, on what Word is the church founded, by what Word does the church live?" Also for Lutheran theology, it is not the law, but the gospel, the message about Jesus Christ, which gathers and gives life to the church.

Furthermore, Lutherans do not insist on preaching the law because it has somehow risen up in our hearts and impressed its authority upon us as a force alongside or in addition to the scriptural word about Christ. Lutherans believe that Jesus Christ is attested *precisely in Holy Scripture* by way of the distinction of law and gospel, so that the church must proclaim the law in order to proclaim Christ *scripturally*. Barmen's one word *contains* the Lutheran two words, or so Lutherans in the Confessing Church argued.[3]

This phrase, "Jesus Christ *as he is attested in Holy Scripture*," is critically important. Article I was aimed at those who claimed that the church hears the Word by which it lives not

---

3. See for example Edmund Schlink, *Gesetz und Evangelium: Ein Beitrag zum lutherischen Verständnis der 2. Barmer These.* Theologische Existenz Heute, Heft 53 (Munich: Christian Kaiser Verlag, 1937). Even though this work, which consists largely of detailed exegesis of the Lutheran Confessions, has in view Barmen Article II, it is thoroughly relevant to Barmen I as well.

only from Holy Scripture but also from powerful movements in society and culture. These so-called "German Christians" would have agreed that the church lives by the word of "Christ." But *their* Christ was a Christ whose identity and meaning were also disclosed in the vital forces of history. Attending to those "other events and powers, figures and truths" was taken to be necessary in order to proclaim Jesus Christ. Therefore the life which Christ came to give had to be somehow linked to the energy that surged upward in the so-called German national rebirth under Adolf Hitler.

To this, Barmen I says, without qualification, *No.* The church does not learn what it must proclaim from such "other events and powers, figures and truths." The article does not deny that there are other significant events and powers, figures and truths in the world. It doesn't even deny that God may be related to these phenomena in one way or another. It provides no theory about God and history. It simply denies that these other phenomena have *authority for the church's proclamation.*

As the Lutheran theologian Hans Asmussen put it, in the address in which he presented the Declaration to the Barmen Synod:

> All these variables cannot restrict the proclamation of Christ, nor can they come forward alongside Christ as objects of proclamation. In proclamation they can have no other place than this: they are signs of the one, basically unchanged world which can find redemption in Christ, but only in Christ.[4]

As Asmussen also pointed out, it is "only a relative distinction" whether events like the Nazi revolution or "reason, culture, aesthetic sensibility, progress" or other powers are

---

4. Hans Asmussen, "Einbringungsreferat," my translation from the text found online at: http://www.ekd.de/glauben/bekenntnisse/einbringungsreferat _asmussens.html.

presented as binding on the church. About all of them it must be said: They may be good or evil; they may be based on truth or falsehood, or more likely, both. But when all is said and done, they are phenomena of the world that need redemption, not powers that redeem.

The Christ to whom the church is called to give its trust and obedience is the unique, particular one whose story is told in the Bible. Jesus is not a symbol that we can manipulate to express our sense of what is important and meaningful; Jesus is the unique crucified and risen Son of God, who has saved us by taking particular flesh and blood for us and surrendering them for us once and for all on the cross. This is what the phrase "as he is attested to us in Holy Scripture" is getting at. The one whom the church trusts and obeys in life and in death is the singular one of whom we learn from the Bible, the one whose singular story is recounted there.

On the way to proclamation, therefore, on the way to mission, the impetus of all our aspirations and enthusiasms must be checked by the fact of the Bible. There is this untidy-seeming collection of texts, written a long time ago, by people who are strange to us, in languages not our own. These texts do not share the assumptions taken for granted in our culture. They don't really answer our questions or offer solutions to what we think our problems are. Yet the confession of the church is that this body of texts has been chosen and prepared by *God* – it is, as 2 Timothy 3:16 has it, "God-breathed."

God has given us these texts in both judgment and mercy: "for teaching, for reproof, for correction, and for training in righteousness." Indeed, the very *fact* of the Bible is already a reproof, a judgment on us; it means that *we are neither the norm nor the source*, that our expectations and aspirations, our felt needs and deep longings give us no access to redemptive truth. But just this judgment serves God's mercy;

God reproves and corrects us in order to clear space in which he can teach us his gospel and form us in righteousness through the Scriptures.

It may seem that I've gone off talking about the Bible rather than my assigned topic, the church. That would be a misperception: the question about Scripture and the church is among the most *profound* questions about the church, because the church is the creation of the Word of God. This first article of the Barmen Declaration reaches all the way down to the church's foundation and spring of life, and warns us against seduction by false authorities, which need not be as wicked as Nazism.

It is actually very easy to drift under the dominion of "other events and powers, figures and truths," besides Jesus Christ as he is attested in Holy Scripture. We have seen how it happens that well-meaning people become caught up in compassionate feelings and the desire to help, and begin to identify the urgency of those feelings and desires with the movement of the Holy Spirit. Then Scripture becomes the problem, the barrier, keeping us from following Jesus. Then good-hearted people find themselves asserting their own attitudes and perceptions *against* Scripture in the sincere belief that they are thereby defending the gospel.

We have seen this, but let us never forget that orthodox, tradition-minded, confessionally zealous Christians can just as easily fall under the sway of such alien authorities. In general, the church is always drawn towards such powers to the extent that it ceases to be a *penitent* community. Whenever we Christians come to be *at ease with ourselves*, whenever we begin to believe that we are *competent* to be the church, then we are ripe for the picking. For example, if we start to feel that we have the gospel handily sewn up in a set of familiar Lutheran slogans, so that we do not need to be constantly learning the gospel from the Scriptures, we will right away begin to fill those slogans with our own easy assumptions and personal preferences.

When that happens, we start to become weary of the Scriptures, which no longer seem to provide anything that we really need. Luther wrote that such weariness with the Scriptures, the bored feeling that we have already done all that, was the great danger to the Reformation church:

> For if any danger hangs over our doctrine, it comes from this vice. The heretics and sects, although they destroy many, at least force us to the diligent study of Holy Scripture. But this deadly disease, distaste for the Word, is born from within us, and it is the more dangerous the less we are able to see it. For it means the certain victory of Satan when we begin to snore, to be secure and sated.[5]

The remaining articles of the Barmen Declaration are really applications of this first thesis to various critical issues concerning the nature and mission of the church.

## ARTICLE II

The Second Article brings forward a point that was already implicit in the First Article in the words "trust and obey in life and in death."

> As Jesus Christ is God's assurance of the forgiveness of all our sins, so also, and with the same seriousness, he is God's mighty claim on our whole life; through him we encounter joyful liberation from the godless bonds of this world to free, thankful service to his creatures.

Having our sins forgiven, as Luther's *Small Catechism* also says, means that Jesus Christ becomes our *Lord*; he has re-

---

5. Luther, Preface to "Commentaries on the Fifteen Psalms of Degrees," *D. Luthers Werke* 40/III (Weimar: Bohlaus, 1930), 12.

deemed us so that we may "belong to him and live under him in his kingdom and serve him in eternal righteousness, innocence, and blessedness."[6]

This coming-under-lordship involves conversion, what the article calls "joyful liberation from the godless bonds of this world." With regard to this, we should not miss the very important contribution that the negative paragraph makes to the teaching of this article:

> We condemn the false doctrine that there are realms of our life in which we belong not to Jesus Christ but to other lords, realms in which we do not need justification and sanctification through him.

This statement has immense implications: *there is no part of our lives over which Jesus Christ does not claim lordship*. There is no aspect of our lives in which we do not need to be justified and sanctified by the Lord Jesus. This means that there is no realm of life in which Christians can simply go with the flow, in which we can just follow the crowd or follow the leader. The "events and powers, figures and truths" that we encounter in the world can never simply be trusted; we can never surrender to them as our lords and masters.

Therefore, we can't simply entrust ourselves to a political movement, however convinced we are that it has the right approach. We can't simply accept the existing ethos of our professions, or the ideas about marriage and parenting and spending that are current among people of our socioeconomic class. We can't accept our job descriptions uncritically; we can't even automatically laugh at the jokes our colleagues and friends tell in the break room. In all these realms, in every realm, we need to be justified and sanctified

---

6. Small Catechism, Third Article of the Creed, in *The Book of Concord: The Confessions of the Evangelical Lutheran Church*, edited by Robert Kolb and Timothy J. Wengert (Minneapolis: Fortress, 2000), 355.

by Jesus Christ. He comes to us there too as those who need his forgiveness and as those whom he claims for his service.

What does this have to do with the doctrine of the church? It means that we cannot close up what happens in the church within some limited realm that we might call "religion" – or these days, "spirituality." The church is not there to meet some need people supposedly have for a "spiritual dimension" in their lives. The church is not a service-provider peddling satisfying "worship experiences" and emotional "wholeness." The church is the agent and witness of the Lord Jesus Christ, who claims every dimension and aspect of human life. The church therefore is by its very nature a community of *disciples*, those who are learning to live under Christ's lordship. The church cannot be the church without catechesis, continuous instruction and formation, and practices of mutual accountability.

Joining the church ought then to be far more *disruptive* than it usually is in mainline Christianity. Joining the church ought to mean that everything in one's life has been opened up for scrutiny and transformation. This is not about the church controlling people; it's about the church proclaiming the scriptural Christ, the Messiah-King who will not be satisfied with less than everything we are. Nor does this imply a slide into legalism: it's *Good* News that we get to have Jesus for our Lord and serve him in his kingdom rather than being captive to the devil. When the church takes discipleship seriously, when it confronts us steadily with "God's mighty claim on our whole life" *in the Christ who is also the assurance of the forgiveness of our sins*, it is helping us to enter into our joyful liberation and preparing us for service to his creatures.

## ARTICLE III

The Third Article then applies the confession of the first two articles to the church's own corporate life:

The church is the community of brothers in which Jesus Christ acts presently as Lord in word and sacrament through the Holy Spirit. With its faith and its obedience alike, with its message and its order alike, as the community of forgiven sinners in the midst of the world of sin, the church has to bear witness that it is his possession alone, and that it lives, and wants to live, solely by his comfort and his instruction in expectation of his appearing.

We condemn the false doctrine that the church is permitted to surrender the form of its message and its order to its own whim, or to changes in the world-views or political convictions dominant at any given time.

According to this article, the church exists because Jesus is risen and Lord, because he lives and acts *presently*, here and now, in bodily space and time. He exercises his risen, active lordship by gathering men and women into a new community through the public proclamation and celebration of word and sacrament. The church belongs to this living, active Lord Jesus Christ – and to him alone. It takes orders from no one else. What was said of believers in Article II is said of the church-community in Article III: there is no realm of its life in which it recognizes any other lord and master.

What rightly challenges Lutherans in this article is the insistence that not only in its *message* but also in its *order* the church must acknowledge Jesus Christ as Lord. Also in the way in which it is organized, the way in which it does business, the church is to bear witness that it belongs to Jesus Christ alone.

Lutherans have struggled since the Reformation with the unfortunate term *adiaphora*, which in Greek literally means "things which make no difference." The issue is the church's handling of matters in its life about which there are no express commands in Scripture. Christ has specified the action that makes up the Lord's Supper and said "Do this!" But there are no explicit instructions about the practical details of the liturgy in which the Lord's Supper is celebrated: the prayers, the hymns, sitting, standing, kneeling, etc. Scripture does not tell us what to do about such things; we have to make decisions. Likewise Scripture does not give us detailed instructions about property maintenance or financial accountability or methods of outreach; in these areas too, the church must make decisions.

The term *adiaphora* is unfortunate because it suggests that it "makes no difference" how we make these decisions; it suggests that the church can indeed act according to its own whim in such matters, or take orders from the "world-views or political convictions dominant at any given time." The "Adiaphoristic Controversy" in the sixteenth century had that temptation at its root, and the *Formula of Concord* insists that at least sometimes it makes a great deal of difference how we make such decisions. Nevertheless, the *Formula* defined the issue rather narrowly, and Lutherans have continued to be tempted to think that it "makes no difference" how the church is governed and organized, how it worships, or how it does business. This has often meant conforming to political and cultural pressures or adopting a thoughtless pragmatism – doing what we think will "work" without stopping to ask "work for *what*?"

Barmen III does not say that there is only one scriptural way of organizing the church, but it does insist that the church's order must *acknowledge the lordship of Christ*. What the church's organization and liturgy and governance must "work" *for* is bearing witness that the church "is [Christ's] possession alone, and that it lives, and wants to live, solely by his comfort and his instruction in expectation of his appearing." This raises questions that we have little practice at asking. What would it be like for a denominational structure or the way parish business is done to bear such witness? How would that affect decision-making structures, or the way we raise money? This challenges us to a new kind of theological thinking, perhaps, a way of attesting the gospel not just with words and ideas but with practices and institutions. For it's not only our words that are capable of denying Christ.

## ARTICLE IV

One issue implicit in Article III is taken further in Article IV:

> The various offices in the church are not the basis for any domination of one over the other, but rather the exercise of the ministry entrusted and committed to the whole community.
>
> We condemn the false doctrine that the church can and may give itself or let itself be given, apart from this ministry, special *Führer* equipped with rights of domination.

The article focuses on the question of *authority* and its legitimate exercise in the church. It denies that power could legitimately be exercised in the church in a mode which it calls "domination," my translation of the German word *Herrschaft*. The German Christians tried to introduce into the church what the Nazis called the *Führerprinzip*, the leadership-principle, according to which the leader embodies the spirit of the people and so the people finds its true self in obeying his commands.[7] This article says No: that is not what a bishop is; that is not what a pastor is.

There are, however, other modes of *Herrschaft* besides the domination of a *Führer*, and this article is indirectly rel-

---

7. On the *Führerprinzip*, cf. Heinrich Vogel, *Wer regiert die Kirche? Über Amt, Ordnung, Regiment der Kirche.* Theologische Existenz Heute, Heft 15 (Munich: Christian Kaiser Verlag, 1934), 30ff. This essay was published in 1934, but apparently written before the Barmen Synod, which it does not mention. Vogel, who taught in Berlin after the war, was one of the most important theologians of the Church Struggle.

evant to those as well. The mainline denominations in the United States spent much of the twentieth century engaged in a great experiment with *bureaucracy* as a form of church order. There is a mode of authority distinctive of bureaucracy, the authority of "the process." In a bureaucracy, when decision-making follows the prescribed sequence of steps, then the outcome claims authority. Bureaucracies tend to resist the idea that their decisions are subject to criticism on the basis of some standard *external* to the process. When a proposal from a church bureaucracy is criticized on the basis of Scripture, for example, the bureaucratic response is typically that consultation with biblical experts was included in the process, so the criticism is illegitimate.

When bureaucracy theologizes about itself, the integrity of its own processes will always emerge as the only serious criterion of judgment. Most of us have heard, in recent years, claims that the gift of the Holy Spirit to the church means that the outcome of the ecclesiastical decision-making process is necessarily the Spirit's verdict. It is a strange modern *Schwärmerei*, for which it is not the spiritual individual or the charismatic prophet but the bureaucratic process itself which has swallowed the Holy Spirit, feathers and all. This is what bureaucracy has in common with the *Führerprinzip*: both the *Führer* and the bureaucracy are a law unto themselves.

Article 28 of the Augsburg Confession maintains that bishops are to rule the church *non humana vi sed verbo*, not by human power but by the Word. Early Lutheran theologians taught that the central exercise of authority in the church was the credible exposition of Scripture according to clear, communally-recognized rules of interpretation. They envisioned a church community in which called and commissioned servants of the Word presided over congregations of catechized and biblically literate laity in such a way that neither pastors nor people "dominated" but both sought together to hear the one Lord of the church in the witness of Holy Scripture. They sought to form church communities in which the heritage of sound doctrine would be treasured, and the foremost concern of both pastors and people would be to preserve intact what they had received from the prophets and apostles and join in *that* confession, not to assert their own enlightenment and creativity in (usually) shallow innovations of their own.

There are no institutional arrangements which can guarantee that the church will be such a community. It would be more in line with the Reformers and Barmen IV to say that it is the central task of the community of forgiven sinners to *strive* persistently to be that community, and in so doing bear witness that it is Christ's possession alone and *desires* to live "solely by his comfort and his instruction" (Article III).

At the same time, institutional arrangements can help or hinder the church in this struggle. In a helpful church structure, for example, authority would arise from the interaction of pastors and people engaging the word of God, whether in local congregations or in assemblies gathered to embody and nurture the communion of the churches with one another. On matters of faith and morals, such assemblies would not simply be the terminal stage of a bureaucratic process, saying Yes or No to proposals developed by "Churchwide." Authority would arise from the assemblies themselves as they sought guidance and instruction from Holy Scripture.

I am the last person to ask for organizational details to fill this out; what I've said is meant only to provoke reflection. As, remember, only a starting-point, the Barmen Declaration can at most stir us to imagine that things could be different, that business-as-usual is not the only possible way for the church to do business. It does so by reminding us that the church is the sole possession of one Lord, Jesus Christ, and that its sole function in this world is to bear witness to him. How are we going to live, if that is who we are?

## ARTICLE V

The last two articles focus on the relationship of the church to the world. The fifth article deals with church and state and is rather long.

> Scripture tells us that the state has by divine appointment the task of caring for the rule of law and peace in the still unredeemed world in which the church also stands, according to the norm of human insight and human capacity, employing also the threat and the exercise of violent force. With thanks and reverence before God, the church acknowledges the benefit of this his appointment. It calls attention to God's kingdom, to God's commandment and righteousness, and thus also to the responsibility of those who rule and those who are ruled. It trusts and obeys the power of the word through which God sustains all things.

In many ways, this is very traditional, but its implications are not at all simple. Let me make three points briefly:

First, *the state stands under the rule of God*. The state gets its authority ultimately from "divine appointment" to a limited task. The political order is neither absolute nor redemptive; it is an institution of the "still unredeemed world." Its specific task is to maintain the rule of law and outward peace in that world. It is for this task and within these limits that the government is authorized to employ violent force. No more than the church, however, does the government have the right to define its task by its own whim or be led by ideology and ambition to overreach itself in ways that undermine the rule of law and destroy peace.

Understood in these terms, the church acknowledges civil government as a gift of God. But notice: it does not say that the church is thankful and reverent towards *the government*. It is thankful and reverent towards *God's appointment*, towards the divine commission that both grants and limits the authority of government.

Second, the central political significance of the church is that *its very existence sets a limit to the state.* "We condemn the false doctrine that the state should and could go beyond its special task to become the single and total order of human life, and therefore also fulfill the task of the church." The state cannot be the single and total order of human life because God has set the church right there next to it, representing a different order, the order of the coming kingdom. The task of the church is to draw men and women under the rule of Jesus Christ into a foretaste of the *final* community, the community of fulfillment, the kingdom of God. If the state attempts to use its coercive tools to absorb everything into a final community of its own devising, then it is trying to be a church; it has gone beyond its commission and exceeded its authority.

Paradoxically, the church is inevitably a political factor precisely because it is *not* part of the political order. The church is a public body in the midst of the commonwealth that cannot be fully integrated into the civil order; it cannot become "an organ of the state." The church exercises its own kind of authority by preaching law and gospel and ordering its own life, in outreach with word and service and the formation of its members for discipleship. This authority of the church is non-coercive but it is nevertheless public and visible, and the government has to come to terms with it.

Third, *the church has a duty to the civil community,* whether government and people welcome it or not: "It calls attention to God's kingdom, to God's commandment and righteousness, and thus also to the responsibility of those who rule and those who are ruled." We might say that the church has the task of telling the state about the real world. The real world is the world to which God is bringing his kingdom, an order beyond the order of the state. In the real world God has given his commandments to humankind and stands by them; it is not wise or healthy for the civil community to despise the commandments of God. The state likewise operates in the world which Jesus Christ is coming to judge; government officials and ordinary citizens alike will be called to give an account to him also of their political lives.

Left to itself, the state does not know these things. It is the task of the church to be the public voice which "calls attention" to them, exercising its own non-violent preaching authority to remind the state of the state's own truth, to teach the state about the real world. The church has absolutely no guarantee about what will come of its witness. It has no program for establishing anything like a Christian regime. It has nothing but the authority that its King claimed when he stood before Pontius Pilate:

> For this purpose I was born and for this purpose I have come into the world – to bear witness to the truth. Everyone who is of the truth listens to my voice (Jn. 18:37).

## ARTICLE VI

The final article says more about the specific mission of the church:

> The task of the church, on which its freedom is founded, is to present the message of the free grace of God to every *Volk*, in Christ's stead and therefore in the service of his own word and work through preaching and sacrament.
>
> We condemn the false doctrine that the church could in human self-glorification place the word and work of the Lord at the service of any sort of arbitrarily chosen desires, goals, and plans.

As we have seen the church does not come into being because religious people get together and found a club. Nor does the church grow in some organic way out of the religious life of the world. The church exists because from his exaltation beyond history the risen Christ exercises his power within history, pouring out the Spirit from the Father's right hand to gather men and women to acknowledge him as Lord and Messiah (cf., Acts 2). The church is therefore never in the position of looking around and wondering what it might best do with itself nowadays. The church is *constituted by its commission*; there is only *one* thing it can do and be the church, just as the Apostle Paul says: "Necessity is laid upon me — woe to me if I do not preach the gospel" (1 Cor. 9:16).

Yet this very necessity, this very pressure of the Lord's commission, gives the church its proper freedom. Because the church is a community under orders from Jesus Christ, it is a free community, free to disregard all the world's self-proclaimed masters. The German Christians wanted to subject the church to the powers at work in the National Socialist revolution. Not everyone at Barmen recognized that those were evil powers, but the Barmen Declaration at least makes this point: the church is not beholden to the powers at work in *any* culture at any place *and* time. The church has no special mission to the German *Volk*; what the church owes the Germans is exactly what it owes to any other *Volk*: the message of the free grace of God.

In our own not-yet-so-extreme situation, churches seem to torment themselves continually about their response to various powers at work in the world. How shall we be relevant to Generations X and Y, how shall we get up-to-date with information technology and social media, how shall we make worship services attractive to people who know nothing of Christianity? Of course we need to learn how to be understood by new generations and diverse populations. But isn't there something strange about the way in which contemporary churches support a whole parachurch outreach-industry that has no precedent in the entire history of the church?

I fear that at least some of our fussing and worrying over these matters constitutes a kind of bondage rooted in a fearful desire for recognition. We want to be important to people, we want be needed. We are disturbed that the church does not have the kind of public respect it once had. We fear for the future of our congregations and institutions. Or perhaps like confused liberals in the 60s, we suspect that "the kids" might be more righteous than we are and so we seek their approval. Of course, this is only a problem because we imagined that we were righteous to begin with, because we imagined that somehow our mission is about *us*, about how *we* are viewed and esteemed in today's world.

In this situation it is liberating, if also embarrassing, to be reminded that the mission of the church really *isn't* about us. It's about the Lord Jesus Christ and the message of the free grace of God in him. We have nothing to offer any generation, age-group, or social class besides "Jesus Christ as he is attested in Holy Scripture." All our freedom, all our worth as a church is located in *him*, in our Head. When we are servants to his word and work through preaching and sacrament, then we truly have dignity and authority, however peculiar or objectionable we may seem to the world: we act in Christ's stead. When our engagement with the world comes to be about us, we immediately become ridiculous, however successful we may seem to be. We become the undignified courtiers and flatterers of this or that accident of history – and we may find that we have sold ourselves to the powers of destruction.

In conclusion, let us hear the words of the Apostle St. Paul:

> God chose what is foolish in the world to shame
> the wise; God chose what is weak in the world to
> shame the strong; God chose what is low and de-
> spised in the world, even things that are not, to bring
> to nothing things that are, so that no human being

might boast in the presence of God. And because of him, you are in Jesus Christ, who became to us wisdom from God, righteousness and sanctification and redemption, so that, as it is written, "Let the one who boasts boast in the Lord" (1 Cor. 1:27-31).

The Barmen Declaration is an invitation to the churches: dare to be foolish, dare to be weak, dare to live in this world knowing nothing but Jesus Christ as he is attested in Holy Scripture – Jesus Christ, and him crucified. Therein is found all the dignity, all the authority, and all the freedom of the church.

## Appendix

### The Theological Declaration of Barmen
### May 1934

#### Article I

*I am the way, the truth, and the life; no one comes to the Father but by me.* (Jn. 14:6)

*Truly, truly, I say to you: whoever does not enter into the sheepfold by the door, but climbs in some other way, is a thief and a murderer.*

*I am the door; whoever enters through me will be saved.* (Jn. 10:1, 9)

Jesus Christ, as he is attested to us in Holy Scripture, is the one word of God which we have to hear, whom we have to trust and to obey in life and in death.

We condemn the false doctrine that the church can and must acknowledge as source of its proclamation still other events and powers, figures and truths as God's revelation, apart from and alongside of this one Word of God.

**Article II**

*Jesus Christ has been made by God our wisdom and righteousness, our sanctification and redemption.* (1 Cor. 1:30)

As Jesus Christ is God's assurance of the forgiveness of all our sins, so also, and with the same seriousness, he is God's mighty claim on our whole life; through him we encounter joyful liberation from the godless bonds of this world to free, thankful service to his creatures.

We condemn the false doctrine that there are realms of our life in which we belong not to Jesus Christ but to other lords, realms in which we do not need justification and sanctification through him.

**Article III**

*Speaking the truth in love, we are to grow up in every way into him who is the head, into Christ, from whom the whole body is joined and knit together.* (Eph. 4:15-16)

The church is the community of brothers in which Jesus Christ acts presently as Lord in word and sacrament through the Holy Spirit. With its faith and its obedience alike, with its message and its order alike, as the community of forgiven sinners in the midst of the world of sin, the church has to bear witness that it is his possession alone, and that it lives, and wants to live, solely by his comfort and his instruction in expectation of his appearing.

We condemn the false doctrine that the church is permitted to surrender the form of its message and its order to its own whim, or to changes in the world-views or political convictions dominant at any given time.

## Article IV

*You know that the rulers of the Gentiles lord it over them, and their great men exercise authority over them. It shall not be so among you; but whoever would be great among you must be your servant.* (Mt. 20:25-26)

The various offices in the church are not the basis for any domination of one over the other, but rather the exercise of the ministry entrusted and committed to the whole community.

We condemn the false doctrine that the church can and may give itself or let itself be given, apart from this ministry, special leaders (*Führer*) equipped with rights of domination.


## Article V

*Fear God; honor the king!* (1 Pet. 2:17)

Scripture tells us that the state has by divine appointment the task of caring for the rule of law and peace in the still unredeemed world in which the church also stands, according to the norm of human insight and human capacity, employing also the threat and the exercise of violent force. With thanks and reverence before God, the church acknowledges the benefit of this his appointment. It calls attention to God's kingdom, to God's commandment and righteousness, and thus also to the responsibility of those who rule and those who are ruled. It trusts and obeys the power of the word through which God sustains all things.

We condemn the false doctrine that the state should and could go beyond its special task to become the single and total order of human life, and therefore also fulfill the task of the church.

We condemn the false doctrine that the church should and could go beyond its special task and take on the manner, the tasks, and the dignity of the state and in this way become itself an organ of the state.

*Lo, I am with you always, even to the end of the age.* (Mt. 28:20).

*God's Word is not bound.* (2 Tim. 2:9)

The task of the church, on which its freedom is founded, is to present the message of the free grace of God to every people (*Volk*), in Christ's stead and therefore in the service of his own word and work through preaching and sacrament.

We condemn the false doctrine that the church could in human self-glorification place the word and work of the Lord at the service of any sort of arbitrarily chosen desires, goals, and plans.

The Confessional Synod of the German Evangelical Church declares that it sees in the acknowledgement of these truths and in the condemnation of these errors the indispensable theological foundation of the German Evangelical Church as a league of confessional churches. It challenges all who can join in its declaration to be mindful of these theological perceptions in their church-political decisions. It beseeches all whom it concerns to return to the unity of faith, love, and hope.

*Verbum Dei manet in æternum.*[8]

---

8. "The word of God abides forever."

# Breaking the Promise of Lutheran Unity:

## Apostasy, Heresy, and Schism

## Nathan H. Yoder

The signatories to the *Book of Concord* declared that in their efforts they were mindful "not to manufacture anything new."[1] Given the abysmal track record of theologians of my generation along these lines – present company excepted – I am now mindful to heed the sage advice Carl Braaten gave me as we parted ways in Canmore, Alberta, after the Canadian Rockies Theological Conference in April 2013: "Don't say anything stupid." Let it be so, *deo volente*.

I begin with a parable of our Lord:

> **25** And behold, a lawyer stood up to put him to the test, saying, "Teacher, what shall I do to inherit eternal life?" **26** He said to him, "What is written in the Law? How do you read it?" **27** And he answered, "You shall love the Lord your God with all your heart and with all your soul and with all your strength and with all your mind, and your neighbor as yourself." **28** And he said to him, "You have answered correctly; do this, and you will live." **29** But he, *desiring to justify himself*, said to Jesus, "And who is my neighbor?" **30** Jesus replied, "A man was going down from Jerusalem to Jericho, and he fell among rob-

---

1. *The Book of Concord* [hereafter cited as BC], ed. and trans. Theodore Tappert (Philadelphia: Fortress, 1959), 13.

bers, who stripped him and beat him and departed, leaving him half dead. **31** Now by chance a priest was going down that road, and when he saw him he passed by on the other side. **32** So likewise a Levite, when he came to the place and saw him, passed by on the other side. **33** But a Samaritan, as he journeyed, came to where he was, and when he saw him, he had compassion. **34** He went to him and bound up his wounds, pouring on oil and wine. Then he set him on his own animal and brought him to an inn and took care of him. **35** And the next day he took out two denarii and gave them to the innkeeper, saying, 'Take care of him, and whatever more you spend, I will repay you when I come back.' **36** Which of these three, do you think, proved to be a neighbor to the man who fell among the robbers?" **37** He said, "The one who showed him mercy." And Jesus said to him, "You go, and do likewise." (Luke 10:25-37, ESV)

We are all more than familiar with this tale, arguably one of the two best-known parables in Christendom (the other being that of the Waiting Father). We tend, I believe, to view it moralistically through a Golden Rule rubric, and chiefly from the viewpoint of the Samaritan, a perspective understandably enforced by Christ's imperative to "go and do likewise." This parable, however, like all the others taught by our Lord, is multidimensional and rich, the *dramatis personae* clothed in layers of truth upon truth.

St. Augustine oriented the scene to include the perspectives of multiple parties, victim and innkeeper as well as rescuer, and his interpretation is beautifully ecclesiological.

Robbers left you half-dead in the road, but you have been found lying there by the passing and kindly Samaritan. Wine and oil have been poured on you. You have received the sacrament of the only-begotten Son. You have been lifted onto his mule. You have believed that Christ became flesh. You have been brought to the inn, and you are being cured in the church. We are performing the duties of the innkeeper. He was told, 'If you spend any more, I will pay you when I return.' If only we spent at least as much as we have received! However much we spend, brothers and sisters, it is the Lord's money.[2]

The Samaritan gives the innkeeper a command, not a request — *take care of him* — along with assurance of the means to do so. The proprietor can comply, or keep the money hidden under his mattress to be doled out for his family alone. Or he can dump the poor devil back in the ditch, forsake his station (in the Greek, *apostasis*, to abandon one's post) and go off arm in arm with the prodigal son to gamble the goods away with the robbers.

But there is yet another character that warrants attention, one whose vocation is similar to that of the innkeeper and whose efforts make possible the victim's convalescence in the inn. If Augustine considers the inn as indicative of the church, I think it is only fair that he extend the same courtesy to the mule, ambulance to the innkeeper's hospital. Guided by the word and operations of its master to the extent that his gesture becomes its action, this noble, ignorant beast bears the burden of bloodied and redeemed sinners along the narrow way. It is both steady and skittish, unpredictably startling at the slightest sound. At points it moves to veer off the path to munch on some bitter shrub, tempted to buck its burden and bolt into the wild.

---

2. *The Works of St. Augustine: A Translation for the Twenty-First Century*, ed. J.E. Rotelle, trans. Edmund Hill (Brooklyn, NY: New City Press, 1990), 3 5:312, quoted in *Ancient Christian Commentary on Scripture, New Testament* Vol. 3., ed. Arthur A. Just, Jr. (Downers Grove, IL: InterVarsity Press, 2003), 180.

I am the son of the son of a farmer. Unlike my father, I haven't had the pleasure of working a plow at the north end of a southbound mule. He tells me, however, that in manning a plow, one has to be watchful of the trace chains that bind the mule to the single trace of the plow, since a mule is ever inclined to slip the chains and step outside the row that is *its* post (again: *apostasis*, apostasy).

On a Lenten pilgrimage to Jerusalem in February 2013 (my first sojourn in the Holy Land), I stumbled upon an ironic scene between Stations V and VI of the *Via Dolorosa*. These are the two Stations of the Cross that best relate to the parable of the Good Samaritan. The first recalls Simon of Cyrene taking up the cross from the Lord, the second St. Veronica's wiping the sweat of his brow when he falls at her feet. There in an alley was a kiosk with a collection of knickknacks of the "my parents went to Jerusalem, and all I got was this lousy T-shirt" variety. Prominent among them was a shirt depicting cartoon men guffawing wildly to the question-caption "Peace in the Middle East?" One of the stick-men was whizzing, Calvin-style, on the word "peace" (for clarification, think Calvin and Hobbes, not Calvin and Zwingli). I was reminded immediately of St. Luke's choice of words in the fifteenth chapter, as the prodigal son *squanders* his father's money into oblivion. The *koine* here has the wonderful advantage of providing *onomatopoeia* to English-speakers: διασκορπιζω (*diaskorpid'zo*) – to squander thoroughly, scattering what has been gathered away, as if into the wind.[3]

We are here today in response to a crisis in Lutheranism, a crisis of the faith. Those who have been entrusted with the Lord's money, the preaching of the Gospel and stewardship of the mysteries, have *diaskorpidzoed* it away by abandoning their posts. In the doing, they have likewise squandered

---

3. *Theological Dictionary of the New Testament*, Volume VII, ed. Gerhard Friedrich, ed. and trans. Geoffrey W. Bromiley (Grand Rapids, MI: Eerdmans, 1971), 421-422.

away any possibilities for Lutheran unity in the foreseeable future.

What is necessary for the unity of the church? We know the answers in the Lutheran Confessions: *For it is sufficient for the true unity of the Christian church that the Gospel be preached in conformity with a pure understanding of it and that the sacraments be administered in accordance with the divine Word* (AC VII.2).[4] We know that the church is the gathering of the community of the Holy Spirit at the Gospel event. We know it to be both holy and sinful, the beloved, dumb, long-eared critter of the Gospel, prone to wander and called to carry. We are reminded by Robert Jenson, still plowing along with us, and Eric Gritsch of blessed memory, that it is the Gospel event – the proclamation, bath, and meal shared by the community of faith – that bears the ontology of the church in Christ Jesus, and not the uniformity of ceremony or polity.[5]

And yet we mourn – not only the squandering of the truth, the doctrinal decay that has brought us to where we are in this 21st-century *Kirchenkampf*, but also the loss of outward, visible unity between our parishes and ecclesiastical bodies. Alongside our mourning comes the temptation to the lawyer's error of wanting to justify himself. Just so, we are tempted to jump into a *diaskorpidzoing* contest of who can outdo whom in breaking the 8th commandment, hurling imprecations like so many horse-apples in the back corral at a 4-H convention. To be sure, the false gospels metastasizing within mainline Protestantism (and in the latest, eager Lutheran additions to it) are indeed indicators of what Carl Braaten has called "the high toleration of heresy and apostasy [that] causes heart failure in the Christian organism."[6] They need to be recognized as such, clearly and soberly.

---

4. BC, 32.

5. Eric Gritsch and Robert Jenson, *Lutheranism: The Theological Movement and Its Confessional Writings* (Philadelphia: Fortress Press, 1976), 126-127.

6. Carl Braaten, *Mother Church: Ecclesiology and Ecumenism* (Minneapolis: Fortress, 1998), 4.

Deviation from the faith has made the current state of separation in North American Lutheranism unavoidable and tragically necessary. But this firm response of the faithful to apostasy in love is one thing. Schism for the sake of antipathy is something else, entirely. Such a motive is schism understood as sin against love[7] – the folly of those seeking Pilate's privilege to wash their hands of the whole sordid matter and withdraw their "righteous" selves from the company of sinners. It is also the sin of those who remain in their respective decaying denominations and proudly wear their dissident status as a badge of honor, all the while disdaining those who have worked to form a new polity, to fashion a new halter for the stubborn creature of the Gospel. Both positions are cases of self-justification. In either instance, we cross to the other side of the path and ignore the suffering of the one dying in the ditch. In the doing, we wander off the narrow way and end up in the ditch ourselves.

"Heretics do not belong to the Catholic Church which loves God," writes Augustine, "nor do schismatics. For the church *loves its neighbor*, and easily forgives his sins because it prays to be forgiven by him who has reconciled us to himself, blotting out all past transgressions and recalling us to new life."[8] Luther follows the lead of Augustine, his mentor in the faith: "[W]here the Gospel is not there is no forgiveness, and hence no holiness. Therefore, all who seek to merit holiness through their works rather than through the Gospel and the forgiveness of sin have expelled and separated themselves from the church" (LC 56).[9] It follows for Luther that those who preach a false gospel are heretics, and those who would justify themselves by separating from sinners are schismatics.

---

7. Van A. Harvey, *A Handbook of Theological Terms* (New York: Macmillan, 1964), 217.

8. Augustine, *De fide et symbolo*, X, 21 (n.p., n.d.), quoted in *The Church: Selected Writings of Arthur Carl Piepkorn*, ed. Michael P. Plekon and William S. Wiecher (Delhi, NY: ALPB, 2006), 23.

9. BC, 418.

Ever watchful of these temptations – and fully conscious that there *will always* be heretics and schismatics within the visible church – the Body of Christ has what Gritsch and Jenson call the "free historical responsibility" to organize structures of polity to safeguard proclamation and sacramental administration.[10] Historical challenges to the Gospel will necessitate changes in polity, and all such structures are provisional. What must remain the same is the Great Commission for which the structures exist, the encounter of the Word of God, the light shining on those who have been in deep darkness and conveying the Good News of restoration and reconciliation. As Luther explains in the *Large Catechism*, "[toward] forgiveness is directed everything that is to be preached concerning the sacraments and, in short, the entire Gospel and all the duties of Christianity" (LC 54).[11] Here is the utter condemnation of self-made satisfactions, whether those of the victim in the parable or the two passersby who are not to be bothered with the Lord's work. Sanctification, bringing sinners to the Lord who feeds and tends them, is the work of the Holy Spirit in the church: the baptismal transfer from ditch to mule, the bumpy ride of daily repentance, and the daily increase in faith and holiness conveyed through Word and Sacrament.

Three connected episodes in the history of Lutheranism in North America – the particular line of Eastern German Lutheranism from whence I come – illustrate the ecclesiological responsibility of change in leadership and polity in response to doctrinal and sacramental crises. Following this historical excursus, we will examine the challenges implicit in responding to heterodoxy within the Body of Christ.

---

Organizational unity among Lutherans in North America has never been a "promise" so much as an ecumenical goal.

10. Gritsch and Jenson, 136.

11. BC, 417.

It was the pious wish of the patriarch of Lutheranism in America,[12] Henry Melchior Muhlenberg, born in 1711, in the city of Einbeck in Hanover. (Einbeck, I have learned, was renowned at the time for sporting over six hundred breweries,[13] a fact that makes me respect Muhlenberg all the more for his willingness to leave hearth and home for the sake of the Gospel!) Muhlenberg's call was in direct response to abuse relative to disorganization. The German Lutherans of the Pennsylvania backcountry were stalwartly independent, having been lured from the Palatinate in southwestern Germany with the promise of farmland along the American frontier.[14] Seeking better lives for their families, they pushed into Pennsylvania because of its policy of religious toleration.[15] From there, many migrated down the Shenandoah Valley and other pathways east of the Appalachians to settle in Maryland, Virginia, and the Carolinas, the very route of my own ancestor. (Conrad *Yoder*, as one might expect, got off the boat holding a Mennonite prayer book. But Heinrich Weidner, the man who recruited the youth to come to Carolina in 1742, was likely a Lutheran, as were a large percentage of those Germans who settled in the North Carolina foothills west of the Catawba River. Conrad's son David eventually followed their example.)

The pioneer impulse of these Pennsylvania Germans, however, did not make allowance for ecclesiastical oversight – they brought no pastors along with them![16] Though aided for a time by the Swedish pastors along the Delaware River, the German settlers soon became prey to itinerant charlatans

---

12. John H. Tietjen, *Which Way to Lutheran Unity* (St Louis: Clayton Publishing House, 1966), 4.

13. David A. Gustafson, *Lutherans in Crisis* (Minneapolis: Fortress, 1993), 36.

14. Abdel Ross Wentz, *A Basic History of Lutheranism in America*, rev. ed. (Minneapolis: Fortress, 1964), 17.

15. Wentz, 4.

16. Wentz, 15.

more interested in serving themselves than being stewards of the mysteries of God. Historian Abdel Wentz calls these men "clerical scamps" and "ecclesiastical tramps," snake-oil peddlers whose leadership was "false and self-serving" and compromised the colonists' love for the church.[17] Thus, when Count Nicolas von Zinzendorf – in Wentz's estimation, a Moravian "posing as a Lutheran"[18] – declared himself the head of the Lutherans in the colony, the Lutheran authorities in Halle, Germany, sent forthwith one of their best and brightest, Henry Melchior Muhlenberg.

It is a testament to Muhlenberg's sheer leadership ability that the 31-year-old who arrived in Philadelphia unannounced and unexpected was able to rein in the Pennsylvania congregations in less than a month.[19] He did this by complementing his authority as a pastor, duly called and ordained according to the Unaltered Augsburg Confession, with the reality of democracy on the American scene, specifically in the governance of congregational business and in the calling of pastors.[20] Though thoroughly confessional, Muhlenberg embraced pulpit fellowship with clergy from other traditions, and he employed a wide variety of worship practices.[21] His aim was for Lutherans in the new world to overcome provincialism and, in his words, "understand the connection and interest of the whole" when it came to being the church, together, and his motto was *Ecclesia Plantanda*, "planting the church."[22]

Under Muhlenberg's guidance, the Pennsylvania Ministerium, the first Lutheran church body in North America, came into being in 1748. It was a small, unapolog-

---

17. Wentz, 15; 37-38.
18. Wentz, 16.
19. Wentz, 37.
20. Gustafson, 38.
21. Gustafson, 39.
22. Wentz, 40; 37.

etically German organization. (While Muhlenberg advocated training in English for the sake of "civic welfare," he saw the German language as instrumental in matters of religion.)[23] But it was a beginning. Following the upheaval of the American Revolution, other synods fell into line: the Ministerium of New York in 1786, and the North Carolina Synod in 1803. It was in North Carolina, the Synod of my baptism, confirmation, and ordination – and the very county of my upbringing – that the first real Lutheran schism on American soil occurred. It proved to be the opening salvo of the American Lutheranism Controversy that would divide Lutherans in the mid-19th century.

By 1820, the Lutheran distinctiveness that Muhlenberg championed was being challenged on multiple fronts by the protestant melting pot of the American frontier. The revivals and camp meetings of the Second Great Awakening were in full force, demanding an outward, emotionally charged personal conversion as the mark of true faith.[24] The so-called "anxious bench" was a regular feature at these services. Folk of questionable moral integrity were rounded up and railed at in an effort to prompt conversion, and known sinners, whether present or absent, were prayed for by name.[25]

[People being what they are, the pious services at the center of these spectacles did not preclude all manner of shenanigans on the periphery. Hence the comment by a fellow North Carolinian to me that, with respect to a local camp meeting that was founded in 1853 and continues annually to this day, there were probably on average "more souls made than saved."]

---

23. Gustafson, 41.

24. Raymond M. Bost and Jeff L. Norris, *All One Body: The Story of the North Carolina Synod, 1803-1993* (Salisbury, NC: North Carolina Synod, ELCA, 1994), 48.

25. Bost and Norris, 51.

This phenomenon of personal conversion is a prime example of what Martin Luther called in his day *Schwärmerei*, religious enthusiasm. (We have the same cognate in English, the ecstatic and collectively oriented "swarming" of bees.) The frontier decision-conversion paradigm does not emphasize God's action in forming faith through the external Word. Instead, outward personal conversion exemplified through personal piety becomes the necessary prerequisite for receiving divine grace.

As Regin Prenter explains in his book *Spiritus Creator* – perhaps the book that best summarizes Luther's theology of the Holy Spirit – the proper path of the Spirit is "the direction from heaven to earth, from God to his creation,"[26] the direction of the Incarnation. The *Schwärmer* stand this order of salvation on its head. For them, it is not God's initiative through his outward Word that actively puts sin to death (what Prenter calls the "theocentric-evangelical" or God-Gospel centered perspective), but the personal decision of the sinner to do so himself (the "anthropocentric-nomistic" or human-law centered focus).[27]

When applied to the parable of the Good Samaritan, this means that the victim must reach out to his rescuer, haul himself up out of the ditch, and climb on the back of the waiting mule. The Holy Spirit thereby becomes a prize to be won, "the crown of the piety of the law, the reward of the perfect, instead of the source and spring of the Gospel."[28] The glorification of personal decision to accept Christ therefore stands in stark contrast to the Lutheran warning against "fanatics who dream that the Holy Spirit does not come through the Word but because of their own preparations"

---

26. Regin Prenter, *Spiritus Creator*, trans. John M. Jensen (Philadelphia: Muhlenberg Press, 1953), 253.

27. Prenter, 254.

28. Prenter, 254.

(AP 13.13).[29] Prenter rightly argues that this kind of enthusiasm is plain old works/righteousness.[30] Though the revivals of the Second Great Awakening emphasized proclamation readily enough, their glorification of personal response rather than God's action in creating faith, as well as their blatant devaluation of the sacraments, places them well under the enthusiasm umbrella.

The Lutherans started to fall in line with the revivalists. Gottlieb Schober, secretary of the NC Synod and a former Moravian (who continued to claim lay status in that tradition, and thus was yet another Moravian posing as a Lutheran), de-emphasized the centrality of the sacraments in favor of personal conversion.[31] Schober was committed to outward Christian unity in spite of inconvenient doctrinal differences. He approved of the Pennsylvania Ministerium's plan of a General Synod of Lutherans in America committed to "unity of sentiment among Christians in general, of whatever kind of denomination."[32] And he praised the Prussian Union of Lutheran and Reformed congregations and hoped that the same policy of union regardless of differences would find realization in North America.[33]

Schober found enormous opposition in a man thirty years his junior who likened the marriage of Lutheran girls with Reformed boys to mating cows with horses[34] – David Melanchthon Henkel. Henkel was thoroughly confessional. In response to the NC Synod's (and thus Schober's) affirmation that "we do not believe that all who are baptized with

---

29. BC, 212.

30. Prenter, 253.

31. Bost and Norris, 57-58.

32. H. George Anderson, "The Early National Period," in *The Lutherans in North America*, rev. ed., ed. E. Clifford Nelson (Minneapolis: Fortress, 1980), 120, quoted in Bost and Norris, 65.

33. Bost and Norris, 57.

34. Gustafson, 108.

water are regenerated and born again unto God," Henkel countered that the Word of God in the water conveys the washing of regeneration and renewal in the Holy Spirit.[35] In answer to the Synod's statement, "we do not believe, nor teach, that the body and blood of our Lord Jesus Christ is corporeally received along with the bread and the wine," Henkel affirmed that it, in fact, *is* so received, "inconceivable by human reason, and divinely mysterious."[36]

Henkel was young and brilliant, only 21 at the time of this interchange. Schober was a former lawyer and a dignitary. The two became fast enemies, ever at loggerheads, Schober determined to prevent the young upstart's ordination. David Henkel's father, Paul, had been instrumental in founding the Synod. Lines were drawn and loyalties established. The formal breach occurred at the 1820 Synod Convention in downtown Lincolnton, North Carolina. Historian Raymond Bost records that in the middle of a heated doctrinal argument, one of the Synod officers declared that whoever considered himself to be a "right Lutheran" could follow him and Schober and their colleagues to a nearby hotel where the real business of the Synod would continue.[37] The response was immediate: "whoever is a real *Schwärmer*, let him follow; for you are no true Lutheran preachers; you are fanatics, and to such you belong."[38] No doubt intended to injure, and thus a clear violation of the eighth commandment, the insult nonetheless carried the virtue of being true.

The ones who stayed – the Henkels and their supporters – proceeded to found the Tennessee Synod, the first Lutheran body in North America founded on doctrinal grounds rather than geographical boundaries. The synod was named for the

35. Bost and Norris, 58.
36. Bost and Norris, 58.
37. Bost and Norris, 46.
38. Bost and Norris, 46-47.

location of its inception at Greenville, Tennessee (where the Henkel party convened a month later), rather than the physical location of its congregations, which were scattered throughout the Southeast. For his part, David Henkel continued to oppose the formation of the General Synod for multiple reasons, one being the absence in its constitution of any points of Lutheran doctrine whatsoever;[39] another (and arguably the main reason for his animosity), that its name in North Carolina was inseparable from that of the man who drafted its initial proposal: Gottlieb Schober, David Henkel's nemesis![40] Whatever Henkel's motives – and they were undoubtedly mixed – his warning against the General Synod's democratic bent rings very close to home.

> Is it possible ... that a majority of votes in our days can prescribe better rules and regulations than those prescribed by Christ and his apostles? ... Can it be supposed that the Holy Spirit, in a miraculous manner taught them without the word? Doth the Holy Spirit, now, teach any person without the word? If this were the case, there would be no need for the word; because everyone might be taught by the Spirit without it.[41]

Some of Henkel's fears were arguably unfounded – for instance, that a general organization would in and of itself compromise the autonomy of local congregations.[42] Nonetheless, the worst of his predictions proved to be accurate, then as now. The core of the General Synod was in sync with Schober's rejection of sacramental theology and traditional Lutheran worship practices. Its policy was doctrinal flexibil-

---

39. Tietjen, 17.

40. Bost and Norris, 63.

41. David Henkel, "Against the General Synod Constitution," in *The Works of David Henkel*, ed. Mark M. Taylor (Fort Wayne: Lutheran Legacy Publishing, 2006), 103-104.

42. Tietjen, 19.

ity,[43] and its champion, Samuel Simon Schmucker, was committed to a pan-Protestant union in the United States as an example to the world, that its churches fall into line together against what he saw to be the global Jesuit menace of the Roman Catholic Church.[44]

Schmucker's brand of "American Lutheranism" called for a "systematic adjustment" of Lutheran doctrine, including an acceptance of free will and a glorification of the human conscience along with a merely symbolic interpretation of the sacraments.[45] For Schmucker, the Lutheran Confessions were no longer binding, and the individual conscience was the final arbiter of belief "in matters not prescribed by the Word of God."[46] Schmucker's *Definite Platform* of 1855, initially circulated anonymously in an attempt to undermine a building resurgence of Confessionalism, included the so-called "American Recension of the Augsburg Confession" and condemned private confession and absolution, baptismal regeneration, and the real presence of Christ in the Eucharist.[47] Rather than stifle the confessional party, the *Definite Platform* was as gasoline to the fire. After another decade of political shenanigans, including walkouts, polemics, jockeying for positions, and general unabashed *diaskorpidzoing*, another schism of American Lutheranism occurred with the formation of the General Council in 1867. Under the leadership of Charles Porterfield Krauth, the General Council followed the example of the Tennessee Synod in forming on a doctrinal basis. Its *raison d'être* is best summed up by Krauth. He writes, "there is no such thing as an 'American Lutheran Church' in any other true and honest sense than this – that

---

43. Gustafson, 56.

44. Gustafson, 69.

45. Vergilius Ferm, *The Crisis in American Lutheran Theology* (New York: Century Co., 1927), 131, quoted in Gustafson, 85.

46. Ferm, 159-160, quoted in Gustafson, 87.

47. Tietjen, 28.

there is an Evangelical Lutheran Church in America, which, in the doctrines of the Gospel and in the right administration of the Sacraments, is *one* with the Evangelical Lutheran Church everywhere else."[48] Those involved in the formation of the General Council thus had a proper handle on the Gospel-event hermeneutic of Lutheran ecclesiology.

---

Each of these three episodes in the history of Eastern North American Lutheranism – Muhlenberg's bloodless coup, Henkel's angry exodus, and Schmucker's sinking ship – shows well the importance of shifting polity and asserting authority in response to doctrinal abuse. The point is not to make heroes of Henkel, Krauth, and Muhlenberg, and goats out of Schober and Schmucker. The former were flawed and sinful servants who nonetheless with their polity renovations made provision for the seven marks of the church: the Word, Baptism, Holy Communion, confession and absolution, the office of the Ministry, prayer, and the way of the cross. The latter party had pious (if misguided) intentions. The last words of Schmucker's *Fraternal Appeal* indicate as much, and we can assume he is genuine: "If this plan is accordant with the Savior's will, may he graciously accept and prosper it; and if not, may he defeat it, and at the day of final account regard with favor the upright intention from which it has emanated!"[49]

But Lutheranism in North America has come a long way from discerning between Henkel's cows and horses. What we are currently facing as stewards of the Gospel is distinguishing chicken salad from other less palatable poultry by-products. The American religious milieu has followed an arguably logical progression from frontier revivalist *Schwärmerei*

---

48. Adolph Spaeth, *Charles Porterfield Krauth*, vol. 2 (New York: Christian Literature Co., 1898), 106, quoted in Gustafson, 166.

49. Samuel Simon Schmucker, *Fraternal Appeal to the American Churches* (Fortress: Philadelphia, 1965), 196.

to full-blown neo-gnosticism, in which the inner desires of the heart are worshipped as direct windows into the divine.[50] Karl Barth prophetically saw this idolatry coming in the 1950s in worship services and lamented how "Reformation praise of God [is] disappear[ing] in the gurgling gullet of modern religious self-confession."[51] Barth called this gnostic navel-gazing "the heresy of the third article."[52] Rather than the Spirit of Christ, it invokes another spirit:

> The spirit of human inwardness and seriousness, the spirit of mysticism and morals. In that spirit we do not yet enjoy, or enjoy no longer, the communion with God which is realized in the revelation of God [i.e., the Word]. On the contrary, for all our seriousness and with all our piety, we are simply alone with ourselves and by ourselves.[53]

Schmucker's dream – God love him – that American Lutheranism would shift with the religious winds of Protestantism has proven true. Where doctrinal indifference was damaging to Lutheran identity before, it is downright destructive to the faith now, and therefore a tool of the demonic. To quote Claus Harms (1778-1855), a German opponent of Lutheran/Reformed unionism, "Lutheranism [has become] reformed into paganism, and Christianity [has been] reformed out of this world."[54] "Mere apostasy" is the designation Robert Jenson ascribes to the current fascination of

50. For a thorough explanation of neo-gnosticism in mainline protestantism, see Carl E. Braaten, "Lutheranism at a Crossroads: Theological Imperatives for the Future," in *Seeking New Directions for Lutheranism: Biblical, Theological, and Churchly Perspectives*, ed. Carl E. Braaten (Delhi, NY: ALPB, 2010).

51. Karl Barth, *Church Dogmatics*, Vol. 1.2, trans. G.T. Thomson and Harold Knight (Edinburgh: T&T Clark, 1956), 257.

52. Barth, 257.

53. Barth, 257.

54. Carl S. Meyer, ed. *Moving Frontiers: Readings in the History of the Lutheran Church–Missouri Synod* (St. Louis: Concordia Publishing House, 1964), 66, quoted in Gustafson, 106.

monkeying with the Triune Name of God.[55] I would extend that category to any alteration of the holy estate of marriage and every other self-affirming symptom of the neo-gnostic gospel of blanket acceptance powerfully resident in mainline Protestantism. I find Jenson's adjective "mere" quite helpful here; not that it in any way attenuates the severity of the charge (it doesn't), but that it speaks to the phenomenon's insidious quotidian, everyday run-of-the-mill character.

-----

Also writing in the 50s, German Lutheran theologian Peter Brunner speaks (again, prophetically) to the gravity of our current situation. The apostolic Gospel and the sacraments are the means entrusted to the church (what Augustine called "the Lord's money") through which God conveys the Holy Spirit, faith, and salvation. Where the Word becomes compromised, faith becomes compromised. Where it becomes completely destroyed – that is, replaced by the witness of the world – then the planting and nurture of faith, the sanctification by the Spirit, becomes impossible.[56] "For the sake of the salvation of human beings," Brunner writes, "the church stands under the commandment to safeguard the apostolic word and with it the unadulterated marks of apostolicity."[57] It is thus in obedience to this command of our Lord to "feed my sheep" (John 21:17), that the church must deny the notion of unity where there is no accord over the content of the Word and the corresponding belief in the ontology of the sacraments.[58]

-----

55. Robert Jenson, "Speech to, for, and about the Triune God," in *Seeking New Directions for Lutheranism*, 111.

56. Peter Brunner, "Die Einheit der Kirche und die Verwirklichung der Kirchengemeinschaft," in Peter Brunner, *Pro Ecclesia* (Berlin: Lutherisches Verlagshaus, 1962), 232.

57. Brunner, 232.

58. Brunner, 232.

Where the Lord's money is *diaskorpidzoed* into the wind, the stewardship of the church requires bold action. It may very well necessitate a separation. Dietrich Bonhoeffer couches this verdict in his condemnation of cheap grace. The sacred responsibility of the office of ministry is the proclamation of the whole Word of God in repentance and forgiveness, Law and Gospel.[59] A communion that refuses to face sin for what it is – that walks over to the other side of the road, yells to the poor devil, come on and get up, you're free, and then continues on its merry way – does not understand the forgiveness of God in Christ Jesus! This is the height of apostasy, of abandoning the cross and thus the portable post we carry with us. Encountering the one who suffers under sin without reaching out in love with the Word of God is inconsonant with what Bonhoeffer means when he says, "when Christ calls a man, he bids him come and die."[60] Such a spirit of carelessness is "unholy," writes Bonhoeffer, as it "squanders the precious treasure of the Lord's forgiveness."[61] Conscientious and tireless stewardship of the Gospel calls for "the daily renunciation of sin and of every barrier which hinders [the disciple] from following Christ."[62] In turning again and again to the reality of our baptism and the forgiveness we have in Christ Jesus, we can spare no part of our lives in faithful repentance. Ignoring this call to repent is tantamount to leaving the trail, altogether.

As the steward of the blessed treasure of the Lord's forgiveness, the innkeeper is to spare no expense, and the stubborn mule can hold nothing back in hauling us sinners along the narrow and rocky path of sanctification. Gross negligence and outright abandonment will necessitate changes in

---

59. Dietrich Bonhoeffer, *The Cost of Discipleship*, trans. R.H. Fuller (New York: Macmillan, 1937), 324.

60. Bonhoeffer, 99.

61. Bonhoeffer, 324.

62. Bonhoeffer, 57.

management. Hence, according to Article 28 of the Augsburg Confession, the Bishops have no authority to institute anything contrary to the Gospel (34).[63] Should this prove the case, Melanchthon provides an answer. "When the bishops are heretics or refuse to administer ordination," he writes in the *Treatise on the Power and Primacy of the Pope*, "the churches are by divine right compelled to ordain pastors and ministers for themselves. And it is the wickedness and tyranny of the bishops that give occasion to schism and discord" (72).[64] Melanchthon lays the blame for schism on those possessing authority. This is not to say that the rest of the church can't be caught up in the resulting spirit of sectarianism – by no means! But as we have seen with Henkel, Schober, Schmucker and Krauth, there is an undeniable connection between heterodoxy and separation. Arthur Carl Piepkorn unveils the etymology of "heretic" to illustrate the point: "sectary," and "division maker."[65] Wolfhart Pannenberg likewise understands the connection between heterodoxy and separation. He defines *heresy* as "concealed apostasy," desertion of the Gospel that may be either willfully or ignorantly adopted.[66]

When is the building so greatly engulfed in the flames of apostasy that the bucket brigade hangs it up and drafts a new blueprint? That is a decision for Christian freedom in response to these concrete challenges to the Gospel. Discerning our historic responsibility to be the church, ever reforming, requires the gift of sound judgment, the courage to act in love on behalf of the neighbor, and above all trust in the Head to whose Body we belong.

The observation that there has never been a time in the history of the faithful that imposters raised up to soothe itch-

---

63. BC, 86.

64. BC, 332.

65. Piepkorn, 49.

66. Wolfhart Pannenberg, *Systematic Theology*, Vol. 2, trans. Geoffrey W. Bromiley (Grand Rapids, MI: Eerdmans, 1997), 414.

ing ears did not hound the church is accurate. But, argues Peter Brunner, there may come a time in an ecclesiastical body when the apostolic Word that divides the error of human supposition from the truth of the living God, Father, Son, and Holy Spirit, becomes so drowned out by the cacophony of the world that the elements of true *ecclesia* within it are virtually silenced,[67] sorely hindering their sacred calling. Within it or without, seeking rapprochement with such a church body by *avoiding* the question of agreement on the apostolic Gospel is nothing less than to contribute to the dissolution of the church.[68]

Concern for the visible unity of the church is truly important: but again, this unity is not the solidarity within institutional bodies but the one life in Christ of the communion of saints across the ages. "Visible" unity is in the end both the transparent fruit of the Spirit and the liturgy of the baptized in bearing and receiving the means of grace. It is the way of the cross; it is narrow, and there is no room for priest, or Levite, or mule, to go to the other side.

Pannenberg points out that the position of unity in the order of essential attributes of the church – one, holy, catholic, and apostolic – is not accidental.[69] For holiness, apostolicity, and universality are impossible without their underlying ontology, the foundation of Christ. "Holiness" invokes the Gospel of the forgiveness of sins and the corresponding imperative to "go and sin no more."[70] "Catholicity" is the universality of the Gospel that is present in each and every particular, isolated gathering of the faithful. In other words, the entire church is present in one congregation's eucharistic worship.[71] And "apostolicity" speaks to the transmission of

---

67. Brunner, 233.
68. Brunner, 233.
69. Pannenberg, 405.
70. Pannenberg, 406.
71. Pannenberg, 407.

the Gospel in Christ Jesus for the forgiveness of sins, the resurrection of the body, and the life everlasting, its witness unbroken from the day of Pentecost.[72] Any invocation to unity must reflect each of the essential attributes, else it is without substance.

---

We have looked at several historical examples of the establishment of new leadership and new structures in North American Lutheranism in the 18th and 19th centuries. Here's one for the 21st. Luther's admonition in *The Power and Primacy of the Pope* has proven to be the case in our current struggle. The Lutheran bishops in North America have either been outright proponents of secularism and neo-gnosticism in the church, or they have to one degree or another dodged the question of real, heretical obstacles to unity in the apostolic tradition. The congregations of the North American Lutheran Church have acted to relieve them and their politically-minded governing bodies of their abandoned posts. This new ecclesiastical body has begun planting the church anew, building provisional and functional structures for the permanent Great Commission of our Lord.

In keeping with AC 28, we have elected a Bishop and established safeguards of theological oversight to:

- declare that a majority of votes cannot overrule Christ and the apostles;

- deny that the Holy Spirit teaches apart from the apostolic Word of God;

- provide for the preaching of the Gospel of the forgiveness of sins in Jesus Christ and the administration of his holy sacraments, confessing that the Holy Scriptures as the Word of God are the norm of our faith and life,

---

72. Pannenberg, 406-407.

confessing the Apostles, the Nicene, and the Athanasian Creeds, and acknowledging the Lutheran Confessions as true witnesses and faithful expositions of the Holy Scriptures.

The Holy Spirit is at the plow, and the mule is breaking new ground. In the event that we in this new church body are tempted toward near-sighted denominationalism – in case we fail to see Muhlenberg's lesson to "understand the connection and interest of the whole" in carrying out our Lord's Great Commission and lose sight of our ecclesiology – Charles Porterfield Krauth's declaration at the General Council's founding still speaks true today: "There is no [North American Lutheran Church] in any other true and honest sense than this – that there is an [Evangelical Lutheran Church in North America], which, in the doctrines of the Gospel and in the right administration of the Sacraments, is *one* with the Evangelical Lutheran Church everywhere else."[73]

The apostolic witness does not sidestep sin and suffering when it proclaims the great exchange that is ours in Christ Jesus alone. We here today, representatives of the "Evangelical Lutheran Church in North America," hold to this imperative to bear the truth in love along the narrow Way. We shine the light of the Lord on unavoidable, concrete situations and persons on our path, on sinners beloved of God, just as sinful and beloved as we are. For this we were chosen from before the foundation of the world. This is the mark of the cross: *kenosis*, emptying, being poor in spirit, and allowing the Holy Spirit to work through our witness to the Gospel.

---

The Tennessee Synod endured for a hundred years when, having run its course of Confessional witness, it rejoined the

---

73. Spaeth, 106, quoted in Gustafson, 166.

North Carolina Synod, which (as a member of the United Synod of the South) merged with both the General Synod and the General Council to create the United Lutheran Church in America. The United Evangelical Lutheran Synod of North Carolina's official history (NC Synod – ULCA) pays the Tennessee Synod the highest praise: "The members of the United Evangelical Lutheran Synod of North Carolina and of the United Lutheran Church in America owe them a debt that can only be paid by a loyalty to the truth which they so valiantly defended."[74] Times and seasons and schisms come to an end. Historical rift can give way to historical reconciliation, and the organizational unity of the church, whether inter-Lutheran or more broadly ecumenical, is no exception. The Holy Spirit has the power to make this happen, and we should not assume that it will take the eschaton for the Spirit to jerk the Body of Christ into line.[75] Peace in the Middle East may yet be accomplished this side of the Kingdom, God willing! We pray the same for the unity of the church.

As to what the organizational circumstance of Lutherans in North America and the world over will resemble in 10, 50, 100 years from now: your guess is as good as mine. I do know there is no shortage of opportunities, formal and informal, for speaking the truth. And the mainline apostasy of the current age may precipitate a Spirit-rich resurgence in ecumenical – and inter-Lutheran – dialogue heretofore unprecedented.

I will leave you with two certainties. The first is an observation concerning justification from Hermann Sasse, warrior in the German *Kirchenkampf* of the 1930s:

---

74. *History of the Lutheran Church in North Carolina*, ed. Bachman S. Brown, John Hall, and Jacob L. Morgan (United Evangelical Synod of North Carolina, 1953), 89.

75. So Carl Braaten in *Mother Church*, 24: "The hope of reunion is not utopian; it is predicated on the knowledge that the sixteenth-century schism was a historical event and, as such, is susceptible of being superseded in the stream of history itself. We do not have to wait until doomsday."

If we stand up for the sinner's justification *sola gratia, sola fide*, it is not the dogmatic idiosyncrasy of a denomination which is at stake, but the article of which nothing can be yielded, even if heaven and earth and all things sink to ruin.... Indeed, it is the greatest contribution which can be made toward the true unity of divided Christendom.[76]

The second is from the ecclesiology of Arthur Carl Piepkorn:

In this world we can hope to know only the church in her present aspect, hated by her foes, betrayed by the false sons within her pale, sore oppressed by the vast number of evil persons in her membership, rent asunder by schisms, distressed by heresies, weeping amid the toil and tribulation and tumult of her warfare. To want to know any other kind of church is presumption, a hankering after a *theologia gloriae* instead of the *theologia crucis* that is our earthly lot.[77]

Take heart, stubborn mule, and trust in the One – Father, Son, and Holy Spirit – who holds the reins.

---

76. Hermann Sasse, *Here We Stand*, Theodore G. Tappert, tr. (New York: Harper and Brothers, 1938), 17.

77. Piepkorn, 49.

# Is Church Order a Matter of Indifference for Lutherans?

**James Arne Nestingen**

Some years ago, Edgar Carlson wrote a classical statement that provides a basis for addressing the question posed. Carlson was serving at Gustavus Adolphus College in a more relaxed period when a college president still had the time to be an outstanding student of Luther and the Confessions. His essay, "The Doctrine of the Ministry in the Lutheran Confessions," was published in *Lutheran Quarterly*. Some 50 years later, it remains one of few definitive references on the topic. Carlson wrote that the peculiar Lutheran tension could[1]

> …be said to be the Word versus the ministry. The ministry in the sense of the whole hierarchy had come to occupy the central place in the life of the church which belongs to the Word, or the gospel. …In Rome ministry presided over the word; in the Reformation view, the word presided over the ministry. …In Rome the Word was an instrument through which the ministry functioned; in Luther the ministry was instrumental to the Word. They were servants of the Word. Through them the Word asserted its living, vital and dynamic character. Therefore, the counterpart in Reformation theology to the hierarchy is not the ministry but the Word. When the Confessions speak negatively, concerning abuses or false doctrines, the focus is frequently on the

ministry…, but when the Confessions speak affirmatively, expounding the doctrine which is asserted, the focus shifts to the doctrine of the Word.

Standing over and against the church and the ministry, the Word does two things. It establishes what is required of both. At the same time, it clarifies the difference between ultimate and penultimate. We'll look at both of these points.

## The Word Establishes the Means of Grace

First of all, the Word establishes the means of grace in the center of both ministry and church. Article V of the *Augsburg Confession*, also commonly called the *Augustana* after its Latin title, *Confessio Augustana*, defines the ministry in terms of the Holy Spirit's work through the means: "To obtain such faith [the faith that justifies, set out in Augustana IV] God has established the office of the ministry, that is, provided the word and the sacraments. Through these the Holy Spirit works faith, when and where he pleases, in those who hear the gospel."[2] Article VII defines the church accordingly as the people of God gathered together to hear the Word and receive the Sacraments.

Speaking of the means of grace, Luther used to say that there is one sacrament and three signs, preaching, baptism and the Lord's Supper. As he makes clear in the *Small Catechism*, the Word is the operative agency in both baptism, which is "water together with his Word," and the Lord's Supper, which is "eating and drinking together with God's Word."[3] To use contemporary terminology, the means of grace are redundant – the Holy Spirit bestows the gifts of the gospel and the faith that goes with them through all three.

---

1. LQ IV, 2 (1963), 120. Jaroslav Pelikan proposed a similar formulation of the tension in *Spirit vs. Structure* (New York: Harper and Row),

2. BC 41, 42..

3. BC 359, 362.

Confession and absolution, the oral declaration of the forgiveness of sins, is passed over in Augustana V and VII. Luther and Melanchthon, his closest associate who was responsible for the final form of the *Augsburg Confession*, saw the confessional – where the Roman Catholic sacrament of penance was exercised by the ministry – as a focal point of abuse. But they did not eliminate it. While they finally concluded that absolution is not a sacrament in the same sense as Baptism and the Lord's Supper, after reforming the practices surrounding confession, they strongly emphasized the importance of both confession and absolution in the life of faith and the church. In fact, two Articles of the *Augsburg Confession* – XI and XXV – are devoted to the retention of confession and absolution in the reforming movement. Even though not formally a sacrament, confession and absolution are clearly means which the Holy Spirit uses for faith.

In fact, later in his article, Carlson points out that in the *Smalcald Articles* – a Lutheran Confession written in 1536-37 – Luther derives the authority of preaching and the sacraments from the absolution. The Reformer writes in Article IV, "God is superabundantly generous in his grace: First, through the spoken Word, by which the forgiveness of sins is preached in the whole world. This is the particular office of the gospel. Second, through Baptism. Third, through the holy sacrament of the Altar. Fourth, through the power of the Keys."[4] Because they convey this superabundance, the means of grace are here extended to include even "…the mutual conversation and consolation of the brethren, "where two or three are gathered." The brethren here clearly include both brothers and sisters. On this basis, Carlson concludes that the preacher's office is defined by the absolution in the same way as a fireman's office is defined by fire fighting.

So the means of grace establishes both ministry and church. Because the Holy Spirit creates faith by speaking,

---

4. BC 319.

there must be a speaker, just as Paul states in Romans 10. So, too, there must be hearers, a community assembled to hear the word set forth from both the text of Scripture and the Altar. The ministry is instrumental to the Word; the church is a creature of Word and Sacrament, brought into being and continued by the declaration of Christ's gifts in oral and sacramental forms.

While establishing both ministry and church, the means of grace also limit it. The faith creating Word is not just any old word, the opinion of the pastor, the latest findings of critical scholarship or the social convictions of an upper middle class determined to incorporate all. It is God's own speech, set out in the comprehensive narrative of the Scripture as both law that restrains and accuses, and gospel, which forgives and frees. By the same token, while grace by its very superabundant nature cannot be contained, constantly overflowing in its goodness, the Sacraments were instituted by Christ himself and are administered under his command. "Go and make disciples of all nations," he said, "baptizing them...." Similarly, on the night in which he was betrayed, feeding his very betrayers, he said, "Do this," that is, gather with me to eat and drink in my Word. The office of keys, which according to John, Jesus committed to his disciples in his first resurrection appearance, authorizes his preachers to speak in his name.

The Confessions use the term "rights" in only one connection. As commonly employed as it is in North American public culture, the conceptuality of human rights developed with the Enlightenment, a century and a half and more after the Reformation. Thus it is not a common interest of the Lutheran Confessions. But Article XIV of the *Augsburg Confession* draws out the strong implication of Articles V and VII – establishing the ministry, creating the church, the means of grace belong to the Holy Spirit who uses them "...when and where he pleases in those who hear the gospel" (CA V), not to the preacher or the church as a whole.

Pastors can claim to serve faithfully only to the extent they are claimed by Word and Sacrament. Thus, Article XIV concludes, "no one should teach publicly in the church or administer the sacraments unless properly called." When the propriety of the call is more fully defined in Melanchthon's "Treatise on the Power and Primacy of the Pope," significantly the congregation, not the bishop, holds the final say. In fact, this is the one point where the Lutheran Confessions speak of a right to the ministry: it is the right of the congregation to be ministered to by the gospel in its preached and sacramental form. "…When the regular bishops become enemies of the gospel or are unwilling to ordain, the churches retain their right to do so. For wherever the church exists, there also is the right to administer the gospel. Therefore, it is necessary for the church to retain the right to call, choose and ordain ministers."[5]

## Ultimate and Penultimate

The language of indifference in relation to church order assumed critical importance at a later point in the development of the Lutheran Confessions, with the *Formula of Concord*. Set out in the face of a victorious emperor determined to enforce the Roman Catholic liturgy to display the unity of his empire, the term *adiophoron* or in the plural, *adiaphora*, still contains an overtone of defiance. The Lutheran estates were not about to submit to force and in Article X of the *Formula*, they entrenched a basis for resistance in no uncertain terms. What Charles demanded as a *sine qua non*, they listed among the options.

In the middle to late 1540s, the political and military alliance that had sheltered the growing Lutheran community

---

5. BC 340.

was compromised. Charles V, who had opposed the Lutheran reform since its beginnings, used the opportunity to strike. The war was over almost as fast as it began. Charles V moved his Spanish speaking troops into Wittenberg, putting himself in a position to enforce terms of settlement that would bring the Lutheran reformation to an end. His own position was precarious, however. Charles had to move quickly to consolidate whatever support he could. For this purpose he set out at least one provisional agreement, an Interim, and possibly another, naming terms that he hoped would bring the Lutherans to the table. One of the provisions was the restoration of the full form of the Roman Catholic liturgy, a demand Charles had carried throughout all prior negotiations with the Lutheran princes. Among other things, liturgical uniformity signaled the political harmony of the empire and beyond it, all of Western Europe – for 16th century Europeans the whole world.[6]

In 1526, citing a form of what later developed into the argument for indifference, Luther revised the Latin liturgy, publishing what became known as the German Mass. Liturgical forms are variable, he said. Besides translating the service into German, Luther made another significant change. He toned down the language of sacrifice, whereby the church obtains merit for the faithful by offering Christ's body to God, and reoriented the service as the proclamation and bestowal in Word and Sacrament of God's gifts in Christ to his people. With the preaching and hymn singing, this revised liturgy became the hallmark of Lutheran worship and a sore thumb to Charles' empirical ambitions.[7]

---

6. For a concise history of the Adiaphorist Controversy, as it is called, see Charles P. Arand, Robert Kolb and James A. Nestingen, *The Lutheran Confessions: History and Theology of the Book of Concord* (Minneapolis: Fortress Press, 2012), 171-190.

7. LW 53, 51-90.

The Lutherans had had to pay attention to issues of resistance since early in the Reformation. They were caught in a dilemma. On the one side, they depended on the support of the political leaders who eventually organized in the Smalcald League; on the other, Luther had been an excommunicant and with his followers placed under the ban of the empire since 1521. Though Luther treated the issue on rare occasion, he didn't really consider it until into the 1530s and then not formally. So after Luther's death in 1546 and the defeat of the Smalcald League in 1547, the whys and wherefores of resistance remained an open question.

Predictably, given all of the other issues that broke open during the later 1540s and early 1550s, the issue erupted in conflict. On the one side, Philip Melanchthon and his adherents argued that since the liturgy involves matters of indifference, the emperor's demands could be accepted as legitimate compromise. On the other side, a brilliant Croatian controversialist who had assumed the Latin name Matthias Flacius Illyricus, argued that when concessions are demanded under threat of force, they are no longer matters of indifference and must be resisted.

Flacius and his colleagues at the University of Magdeburg, where he was for a time a member of the faculty, thought through the whole issue of resistance. Their proposal remains a signal contribution to the Lutheran Reformation. It stands in the background of Article X of the *Formula of Concord*, which formally settled the dispute. Article X employs the terms *adiaphoron* and *adiaphora*, the formal language of indifference, over and against efforts to impose forms in the liturgical and political life of the church that are not set forth in Scripture.

If naming the issues involving matters of indifference casts the discussion in the negative as mere options, Article VII of the *Augsburg Confession* – the first full confessional statement on the matter – declares the original combination by stating the positive basis before moving to what it disallows. "It is enough for the true unity of the Christian church that the gospel is preached harmoniously according to a pure understanding and the sacraments are administered in conformity to the divine Word." This sets the basis for the negative: "It is not necessary for the true unity of the Christian church that uniform ceremonies, instituted by human beings, be observed everywhere."[8]

The gospel pronounces the ultimate. In Christ Jesus, God has taken on flesh to restore the earth and its people, confronting the powers of death, deceit and disruption to make the earth the garden he created it to be. The forgiveness of sins, deliverance from death and the devil, the resurrection of the dead – the gifts of the gospel bestowed by Christ Jesus – give entry to the new creation. Everything depends on this word, in the power of the Holy Spirit, being declared to any and all – every nation.

In this light, the light of the gospel, matters of church life and practice appear as matters of indifference, peripheral to the center. They are penultimate, matters which members of the community can consider in their time and place, making the decisions that they consider appropriate.

The liturgy is certainly included among the matters of indifference in this sense. The gospel itself, as the last word, sets down the standard for the other words, no matter how traditional or novel they may be, which the church uses to proclaim it. American Lutherans have used the freedom this distinction provides to make a series of liturgical revisions. *The Service Book and Hymnal*, the old red book, gave way to Eugene Brand's *Lutheran Book of Worship*, which attempted on the basis of earlier liturgical traditions to correct the Reformation's forms. The ELW, the new red book or "the Cranberry," with its proliferation of options apparently seeks

---

8. BC 42.

to enclose every possibility. With all of this messing around, confessional Lutheran congregations may very well find the best option of all in Missouri's *Lutheran Service Book*.

It may appear to be something of a stretch to include church order under Article VII's use of the term ceremonies. But in fact, the same freedom evident liturgically broke out and has been sustained politically, in Lutheran organizational forms. This is in marked contrast to Roman Catholics, on one side, and Protestants, on the other, both with heavy commitments to ecclesiastical structures. The gospel reduces church order to a penultimate consideration. So Lutheran churches have historically taken a variety of forms, from the state and folk churches of Germany and Scandinavia, from episcopal forms of governance to the American free churches. The bishops' betrayals in the 16th century made such a deep impression that it took more than four centuries and an ocean crossing before American Lutherans could use the term "bishop" freely. It is commonly observed that when we started calling them bishops, they thought they were, but even such remarks indicate the acceptance, however reluctant it may be, of the bishops as part of the larger variety of alternatives.

It is important to note, however, that while the gospel as the last word renders penultimate both liturgical forms and matters of church governance, in the down to earth connections of everyday life they still hold importance. It took nearly a millennium for the church to turn the sacrament to a sacrifice, but for all the power of the biblical and confessional critique of sacrificial thinking,[9] superstitions still stalk the liturgy. Whatever their value, the new liturgies generally appear to have shifted the action from Christ Jesus to the faithful, who put themselves forward as acting for him. By the same token, when political forms are rendered optional, the already

---

9. BC 259-261.

powerful quickly step in to supervise. Thus law and reason have to have their place, precisely because matters of indifference may turn out to be decisively destructive. While the gospel relativizes, it does not eliminate that which supports its proclamation in the human community.

# Whether Church Order Is a Matter of Indifference in Lutheran History and Theology

**Frank C. Senn**

irst let me define "church order." As a liturgist I've spent a lot of time with the genre of primary documents known as church orders: first in the ancient church and then in the Reformation era. The earliest church order we know of is the *Didache* (*The Teaching of the Twelve*), which dates from the end of the first century and represents the practices of a Jewish Christian community. The interesting thing is that the kind of topics dealt with in the *Didache* are also dealt with in later church orders, both in antiquity and in the Reformation era.

The content of the *Didache* includes: a catechism (the Way of Life and the Way of Death – much of the material drawn from the Gospel of Matthew); Baptism (including how to fast and how to pray – the Trinitarian baptismal formula is the same as in Matthew 28:18 and the text of the Lord's Prayer is based on Matthew's version); the Eucharist (including table prayers, but no words of institution); hospitality (the reception of itinerant apostles and prophets and other traveling Christians); the distribution of food and clothing and other material needs; confession and reconciliation; the election of bishops; church discipline; and an eschatological conclusion.[1]

---

1. See Kurt Niederwimmer, *The Didache: A Commentary*, trans. Linda M. Maloney (Minneapolis: Fortresss Press, 1998).

The second oldest church order may be *The Apostolic Tradition* attributed to Hippolytus of Rome. It used to be dated in the early third century in Rome, but recent scholarship has called into question just about everything we assumed about this church order, including time, place, and authorship. But, again, the content is similar to what appears in other church orders: directions for the election and ordination of bishops (including the ordination prayer, a eucharistic prayer for the new bishop to use, and offerings at the Eucharist), presbyters and deacons; the appointment of confessors, widows, readers, virgins, sub-deacons; the recognition of healers; the rites of Christian initiation from enrollment and the practices of the catechumenate through baptism, sealing, and first communion; the care of the sick; the shared meals of the congregation (this is still in the era of house churches); times of prayer; communion practices; the sign of the cross and other miscellaneous items.[2]

Not only are items included in the *Didache* and *The Apostolic Tradition* also included in later church orders, but material is lifted from them and edited. We are dealing here with what Paul Bradshaw called "living documents." The materials of the ancient church orders are preserved in Greek, Latin, Syriac, Coptic, Ethiopian, and Arabic. It's like the succession of hymnals in which texts are translated from one language into another and then are altered from one generation to the next. Liturgical documents are not static because Christian communities are not static and even historical material must be the prayer of the contemporary assembly. Liturgy is not a book, it is what the church does when it comes together before the Lord.

Now we jump to the sixteenth century. If the ancient church orders represented the development and organization of church practice, the Reformation church orders rep-

---

2. See Paul F. Bradshaw, Maxwell Johnson, L. Edward Phillips, *The Apostolic Tradition: A Commentary* (Minneapolis: Fortress Press, 2002).

resent the renewal and re-organization of church practice. Martin Luther's treatises on the *Form of the Mass and Communion for the Church at Wittenberg* (1523) and *German Mass and Order of Service* (1526) can be considered proto-Reformation church orders. The church orders are not worship books or agendas; they give the order of service with commentary on what to use from existent books. They provide liturgical texts only where changes were to be made from the existing orders. In the German Mass Luther included music for the German texts that replaced the Latin texts. He even provided practice exercises for pastors to learn how to chant the collects, Epistles and Gospels in German. He included directions on how to receive communion.

Probably the first full church order was a Hessian Church Order that appeared in 1526. It was sent to Luther for his evaluation, and he didn't much like it because it seemed like a return to canon law. But then in 1528 Luther aided Philip Melanchthon in drawing up *Articles for Parish Visitors* for Electoral Saxony as official visitors were sent under the authority of His Electoral Grace John the Steadfast in the absence of visitation by the bishops. The Visitation Articles included a check list of things to look for in parish life. These items would become the topics of concern in the Evangelical church orders. We know that Luther's own experience as a parish visitor opened his eyes. He prepared his Large and Small Catechisms as a response to the dilapidated state of Christian knowledge and religious life found in the visitations.

In the meantime, Luther's pastor at Wittenberg, Johannes Bugenhagen, was loaned by the elector of Saxony to rulers across northern Germany and the kingdom of Denmark and Norway to prepare church orders for these territories and realms. Johann Brenz became involved in drafting church orders in southern Germany. Melanchthon was also a consultant in the drafting of church orders. His most notable collaboration was with Martin Bucer of Strasbourg on a church order for the Elector-Archbishop Hermann von Wied of Cologne in 1543, which was translated into English as *A Pious and Religious Consultation* and became an important source of *The Book of Common Prayer*. Pastor Andreas Osiander prepared an important church order for the city of Nürnberg in 1533, which was also seen by the future archbishop of Canterbury, Thomas Cranmer, who was serving as King Henry VIII's ambassador to the Holy Roman Empire when Charles V was holding court in Nürnberg in 1532-33. Cranmer also had a copy of Osiander's Catechism and Order of Baptism and he married Osiander's niece. So Cranmer's Lutheran connections were rather extensive and are reflected in the *Book of Common Prayer*.[3]

The Nürnberg Church Order served as the basis of the Mark Brandenburg Church Order of 1540, which differed mostly in being more conservative liturgically. The church orders or ordinances replaced canon law and therefore had to deal with some issues that had been covered in medieval canon law, such as laws regulating marriage.

In all about 135 church orders were produced in Germany and other Lutheran lands during the sixteenth century.[4] These were official ordinances of the cities and realms that adopted the Reformation and established it in law. Books of Discipline were comparable documents in the Reformed Churches in Geneva, Scotland, and The Netherlands. Each church order was intended for local use, so there was some variation among them, especially in matters of liturgy and polity. But there was also a great deal of borrowing from one to another, as in the ancient church orders. They covered similar topics, including standards of belief and doc-

---

3. The *Book of Common Prayer* in the Anglican tradition combines elements of agenda, confession, and church order found in early Lutheranism.

4. The church orders have been collected in Emil Sehling, ed., *Die evangelischen Kirchenordnungen des XVI. Jahrhunderts*, Vols. 1-5 (Leipzig, 1902-1913); Vols. 6- (Tübingen, 1955- ).

trine, reforms associated with worship, and administrative concerns which included church polity, church discipline, marriage laws, and social welfare, such as the establishment of the common chest, hospitals, and orphanages to replace begging and the monasteries, which were quickly being emptied out and dissolved.

One of the most unusual church orders was the Swedish Church Order of 1571 (*Den svenska kyrkoordning*), which also covered Finland. The main drafter of this ordinance was the archbishop of Uppsala, Laurentius Petri, who had been archbishop since 1531. (He was the brother of Sweden's main reformer, Olavus Petri – both Peterson brothers had studied in Wittenberg.) As the Reformation made its way in Sweden by fits and starts, Archbishop Lars had tried in vain to persuade kings Gustav Vasa and Eric XIV to be allowed to publish a complete church ordinance. With the accession of King John III in 1568, Petri was granted permission, and in 1571 he published *Canon Ecclesiasticus*.[5] It was formalized at a church meeting in 1572. By this action all the fundamental Lutheran doctrines were affirmed and medieval canon law formally lost its authority in Sweden. The archbishop's work was marked by a profound compromise between the old and the new. He altered the Catholic doctrines that he believed were incompatible with true Christianity, but allowed others to remain if he deemed them useful. Probably the most noteworthy feature was the retention of the historic episcopate, even though it was not directly mandated by holy Scripture. But he noted that the distinction between bishop and priest "...proved useful and without doubt was inspired by God the Holy Spirit, from whom all good gifts come," so that "it was approved and accepted in all Christendom. Thus it came to be, and must be as long as the world lasts."[6] The chapter on

5. See *Den svenska kyrkoordningen 1571*, ed. Sven Kjöllerström (Lund, 1971).

6. Cited in Conrad Bergendorf, "The Unique Character of the Reformation in Sweden," in *Symposium on 17th Century Lutheranism* (St. Louis: Concordia Publishing House, 1962), 98.

Penance, Confession and Absolution provided for public penance as well as individual confession. The chapter on the Lord's Supper expressed a positive understanding of the eucharistic sacrifice. And the Order of Mass allowed for the elevation of the host and chalice and prescribed kneeling to receive communion. The late venerable Conrad Bergendorf commented,

> ...the Swedish situation revolved around public practices which involved a theology, and the defense of elevation and veneration proclaimed the reality of Christ's presence as surely as any scholastic subtleties. The people understood little of *communicatio idiomatum*, but they did understand that the sacrament was more than a memorial of a symbol if the cup was elevated and the proper posture was kneeling.[7]

We should consider that for ordinary people, then as now, the way to the mind is through the rest of the body, including the senses and postures. The same situation pertained in early seventeenth century Brandenburg when the House of Hohenzollern embraced the Calvinist confession while most of the people remained Lutherans. The people knew whether a Lutheran or a Reformed pastor was being sent to them by whether the pastor elevated the bread or broke it. Bread-breaking pastors could be unceremoniously lifted up and escorted physically out of the church building.[8]

The church orders were obviously very important documents in the progress of the Reformation. One could say that they were important alongside the Confessions. In fact, the church orders also included confessional elements just as the Confessions include elements of agenda or practice that

---

7. *Ibid.*, 96.

8. See Bodo Nischan, *Prince, People, and Confession: The Second Reformation in Brandenburg* (Philadelphia: University of Pennsylvania Press, 1994), 47-49, 64-67, 139-41.

were included in the church orders. The only real difference between them was that the Confessions acquired an international status whereas the church orders were intended for local use. But the two went together. In 1593 when Sweden-Finland had to prepare for the accession of Johan III's son Sigismund III Vasa, who was already king of Poland and a champion of the Counter-Reformation, a national synod was convened in which the Church Order of Laurentius Petri was re-adopted as a standard of practice and, for the first time, the *Augsburg Confession* was adopted as a standard of belief. These documents were set before Sigismund as the standards of the faith and practice of the Church of Sweden.

As the post-Reformation age of orthodoxy settled in, Lutheran pastors could no more deviate from the church orders than they could depart from the Confessions to which they subscribed in their ordination vows if they held a pastoral office.

I wanted to set this situation before you as we consider the question of "whether church order is a matter of indifference in Lutheran history and theology." "Matters of indifference" are called *adiaphora* in the Lutheran confessions. That's a term you lay people should know so you can throw it around like the pastors do. So learn what *adiaphora* means: "indifferent matters."

Next I want to suggest that *adiaphora* is one of the least helpful categories ever imported into Lutheran theology.

I suppose some such category is necessary to distinguish between what is essential from what is not essential to Christian faith and life, and that is important in order to demarcate areas of Christian freedom. A famous example is the situation St. Paul addressed to the Corinthians about eating food sacrificed to idols. Some said they could eat such food because the gods to whom the food was offered were not real. But these gods were probably real enough to recent converts, who might be put into "bad faith" if their fellow believers ate what they abstained from. In response, Paul replied: "...food does not bring us near to God; we are no worse if we do not eat, and no better if we do. Be careful, however, that the exercise of your freedom does not become a stumbling block to the weak" (1 Corinthians 8:8-9 NIV). So maybe it is not a matter of indifference whether one eats such food just to be sociable with one's pagan neighbors.

We run into the same situation in Lutheranism. The issue of what constituted *adiaphora* became a major dispute in 1548. Two years after Luther's death and the defeat of the Lutheran princes of the Smalcald League in the Smalcald War after the defection of Elector Maurice of Saxony, the Emperor Charles V tried to unite Catholics and Protestants in the Holy Roman Empire with a law called the Augsburg Interim. The idea was to reimpose some Catholic practices in the defeated Lutheran territories until these issues could be decided by an ecumenical council. This law was rejected by Melanchthon because it did not ensure justification by faith as a fundamental doctrine. Later he was persuaded to accept a compromise known as the Leipzig Interim, after deciding that doctrinal differences not related to the article on justification by faith were *adiaphora* or matters of indifference. Melanchthon's compromise was vehemently opposed by Matthias Flacius and his followers in Magdeburg, who went to the opposite extreme by claiming that *adiaphora* cease to be "indifferent matters" when faith is being challenged. So the adiaphoristic controversy was born.[9]

By 1577 both extremes were rejected by the majority of Lutherans led by Martin Chemnitz and the formulators of the *Formula of Concord*. Among other controversies the

---

9. See Eric W. Gritsch and Robert W. Jenson, *Lutheranism: The Theological Movement and Its Confessional Writings* (Philadelphia: Fortress Press, 1976), 191-206.

*Formula* settled the question of the nature of genuine *adiaphora*, which it defined as church rites that are "...neither commanded nor forbidden in the Word of God." However, the *Formula* added that believers should not yield even in matters of *adiaphora* when these are being forced upon them by the "enemies of God's Word." The celebrated Latin phrase is: *Nihil est adiaphoron in statu confessionis* – "nothing is an indifferent matter in a situation of confession."

So those good Lutheran burghers in Berlin in the early seventeenth century could not tolerate a Reformed pastor breaking the bread instead of elevating it when the doctrine of the real presence of Christ was at stake. The *fractio panis*, neutral enough in other circumstances (and even Jesus "broke the bread" when he "took" it!), must be rejected in a state of confession. And the elevation of the host, long abandoned in other Lutheran territories, must be restored in a grand ostension when your pastor is teaching that Christ is in heaven and not on the earthly altar.

Where does that leave us? *Adiaphora* are "indifferent matters." What is an essential matter? What is essential is what pertains to our salvation. But God has taken care of our salvation in the saving act of the atoning sacrifice of Jesus Christ, the Son of God. That is the gospel and its consequence is that we are justified by faith alone in Christ alone as testified in Scripture alone through the means of grace alone.

That's essential. Everything else is left to the free decision of the church. Everything else is an *adiaphoron*. Except when some confessing must be done. Then *nihil est adiaphoron* – "nothing is an adiaphoron." It's helpful if the church defines what "a state of confession" is, as the Lutheran World Federation did with apartheid in South Africa. Otherwise we are left to our own lights about whether the faith is being challenged or not. If it is, then the most seemingly inconsequential thing cannot be an indifferent matter.

So you see that the concept of *adiaphoron* is not very helpful. It's an all or nothing category, which is not where most of us find ourselves most of the time. The usual result has been that if something is considered "a matter of indifference," people don't consider it at all. In the ethos of American pragmatism, when it comes especially to matters of worship, our tendency is to do whatever seems to work, with little regard for what we are communicating to the faithful. So we either do whatever we have been doing or whatever new thing is coming down the pike, and if the people are content, the pastor is content. We adopt practices of church organization in the same way: we do whatever works to get the job done. This usually means adopting the organizational principles of business corporations, without considering that this cultural model, like all cultural expressions, comes imbued with a particular world view and value system.

On the other hand, there are pastors and bishops with a persecution complex who are always ready to go to war over any and every little detail of liturgical ceremony and constitutional rules. I dare say that a lot of opportunities for bridge-building (aren't bishops supposed to be pontiffs – bridge builders?) have been squandered by ELCA bishops who hurled the ELCA Constitution at disgruntled congregations instead of reaching out to them with love and in understanding.

Is there another way to proceed that avoids the all or nothing approach? Well, actually there is. It is the way of tradition. Carl Braaten didn't ask me to talk about this, but I'm going to talk about it anyway because it is also a confessional category that gives us a way of dealing with matters of church order that is not all or nothing. The praeceptor of Germany, Master Melanchthon, who introduced the concept of adiaphora into our theological thinking also gave us the category of *traditiones* or *Menschensatzungen* – "human traditions."

Luther himself set the tone for valuing tradition in his *Form of Mass* 1523 when he stated: "It is not now nor ever has been our intention to abolish the liturgical service of God completely, but rather to purify the one that is now in use from the wretched accretions which corrupt it and to point out an evangelical use."[10] Apart from his radical surgery on the offertory and eucharistic prayers, much of the rest of the Mass – and the orders of Matins and Vespers – were left intact. Melanchthon testified to the emerging evangelical practice in Article 24 of the *Augsburg Confession* when he stated, "We are unjustly accused of having abolished the Mass. Without boasting, it is manifest that the Mass is observed among us with greater devotion and more earnestness than among our opponents. ... Meanwhile, no conspicuous changes have been made in the public ceremonies of the Mass, except that in certain places German hymns are sung in addition to the Latin responses for the instruction and exercise of the people."[11] *The Apology* Article 24 amplifies that. "In our churches Mass is celebrated every Sunday and on other festivals, when the sacrament is offered to those who wish for it after they have been examined and absolved."[12] Article 15 of the *Augustana* states, "With regard to church usages that have been established by men, it is taught among us that those usages are to be observed which may be observed without sin and which contribute to peace and good order in the church, among them certain holy days, festivals, and the like."[13] Article 15 in the *Apology* introduces the terms *Traditionibus humanis* and *den menschlichen Satzungen* – "human traditions."

---

10. Martin Luther, "An Order of Mass and Communion for the Church at Wittenberg," *Luther's Works*, 51, ed. Ulrich S. Leupold (Philadelphia: Fortress Press, 1965), 20.

11. Augsburg Confession, 24; *The Book of Concord*, ed. Theodore G. Tappert (Philadelphia: Fortress Press, 1959), 56.

12. Apology of the Augsburg Confession, 24; *ibid.*, 249.

13. AC, 15; *ibid.*, 36.

Before I comment at greater length on the concept of tradition, let me first note that some issues of church order can never be considered an *adiaphoron* or human tradition. One is the office of the ministry. According to Article 5, the office of the ministry is of divine institution; God instituted the office of the ministry when he provided the Gospel and the Sacraments. Moreover, Article 14 states that "nobody should publicly teach or preach or administer the Sacraments in the church without a regular call." The *Apology* testifies "to our deep desire to maintain the church polity and various ranks of the ecclesiastical hierarchy, although they were created by human authority."[14] In some places, notes Melanchthon, the evangelical church has had to abolish the canonical church government, "despite our earnest desire to keep it," because the bishops force our priests to forsake our teachings or they kill them.

Also, the Sacraments cannot be considered *adiaphora* or human traditions because they are also of divine institution. The church has the command to baptize in the name of the Father and of the Son and of the Holy Spirit. The church has the command to take bread and wine, give thanks over them, and distribute these elements to be eaten and drunk for the remembrance (*anamnesis* – reactualization) of Christ. The church also has the command to forgive or retain sins and thereby to exercise the office of the keys. How these Sacraments are administered is left to the church, and those decisions are contingent on many factors, such as the time and place of assembling and the number of people in the assembly and the availability of ministers to exercise the office of preaching the Word and administering the Sacraments. But the means of grace are not indifferent matters.

By the instruction of our Confessions the church will be guided by tradition in ordering the ministry and arranging for the preaching of the Word and the administration of the

---

14. AC, 14; *ibid.*

Sacraments. The *Augsburg Confession* and its *Apology*, taken together, indicate a high regard for human traditions in the church as a principle for making decisions about church order. Traditions were valued by Luther and Melanchthon out of pastoral and ecumenical concerns. They didn't want to put people in bad faith through reckless change and they wanted to preserve Christian unity. What is lacking in Melanchthon's argument, but which we saw in Laurentius Petri's, was an appeal to the work of the Holy Spirit in the history of the church. Luther taught in his Catechism that the holy Christian church is "called, gathered, enlightened, and sanctified by the Holy Spirit." Therefore, as the apostles said after their council meeting in Acts 15, some practices are embraced because "they seem good to the Holy Spirit and to us." It is a matter of respecting the *consensus fidelium* (the consensus of the faithful) brought about by God the Holy Spirit in the life of the church, which is the Spirit's creation.

We come closer to that foundation for the role of tradition in the life of the church in Martin Chemnitz's monumental *Examination of the Council of Trent* (1565-1573). We recall that Chemnitz was one of the authors of the *Formula of Concord* and of the completed *Book of Concord*. The concern for tradition was transparent in the *Book of Concord*. The three ecumenical Creeds were the first documents included in the Book so that the *Augsburg Confession* was construed as a commentary on the ecumenical Creeds. A Catalogue of Testimonies of the Fathers (*Testimonia Patrem*) was appended to the *Book of Concord*.

The whole of Chemnitz's *Examination of the Canons and Decrees of the Council of Trent* was conducted by a dispassionate appeal to Scripture and tradition. But in the first volume he distinguished between eight different senses in which the term "tradition" is used.[15]

---

15. Martin Chemnitz, *Examination of the Council of Trent*, Part 1, trans. Fred Kramer (St. Louis: Concordia Publishing House, 1971), 271-307.

1. Those things which Christ and the apostles handed down in a living voice as oral tradition that were subsequently committed to writing – in other words the Scriptures themselves.

2. The transmission of the Sacred Scriptures by hand from one copy to another.

3. Irenaeus and Tertullian celebrate the apostolic tradition in articles of faith that are known to us today as the Apostles' Creed.

4. The interpretations of texts of Sacred Scripture which have been handed down from the fathers.

5. Dogmas that are not set down in Scripture in so many words, but which are drawn from clear passages of Scripture, such as original sin, the two natures of Christ, the Trinity.

6. The catholic consensus of the fathers on matters of faith and morals.

7. Ancient rites and customs which, because of their antiquity, are referred to as apostolic. Chemnitz gives such examples as the sign of the cross, turning to the east for prayer, "the words of the epiclesis when the bread of the Eucharist is shown," the blessing of the font, the baptismal anointing, the three-fold immersion, the renunciation of Satan, the confession of faith, etc. Concerning these traditions Chemnitz writes, "We do not simply reject and condemn all traditions which are of this kind. For we do not disapprove of what Jerome writes to Lucinius, namely, that the churchly traditions, especially such as do not harm the faith, are to be observed as they were handed down by the elders."[16]

---

16. *Ibid.*, 271.

8. Unwritten traditions pertaining to faith and morals that the Council of Trent accorded an equal dignity to the Scriptures themselves "and which cannot be proved with any testimony from Scripture."[17] Only this last understanding of tradition is rejected.

The role of tradition in preserving or recovering catholic church order is formidable in Lutheran history and theology. There is an intrinsic relationship between faith and practice, doctrine and agenda. The confessional revival in the nineteenth century, after the age of Rationalism, was accompanied by liturgical retrieval (seen, for example, in the Common Service of 1888), and also by the restoration of the office of bishop, first in Europe and then in North America. There is no guarantee that the Trinitarian and Christological orthodoxy affirmed in the ecumenical Creeds and pervading the Lutheran Confessions and the historic liturgies will be preserved in revisionist and contemporary liturgies. Teaching authority (*magisterium*) is no more secure if a church leader is called a bishop than if he or she is a church president. But it might help if Apology 28's distinction between the temporal and spiritual authority of the bishop is applied to our American situation and all temporal authority is removed from the office of bishop so that only spiritual authority is left when bishops visit congregations to preach the Gospel, administer the Sacraments, provide counsel, and administer discipline. The corporate managerial model of leadership must be eschewed.

We gather in these CORE theological convocations because we believe that the very basics of the faith are up for

---

17. *Ibid.*, 273. Chemnitz cites from Peter a Soto such items as the offering of the sacrifice of the altar, the invocation of the saints, the merits of works, the primacy of the Roman pontiff, etc. "in order that the reader may see that the controversy in this discussion about traditions [in this sense] is not about indifferent things but about matters of the greatest importance."

grabs today. I need mention only two major ones – the doctrine of the Trinity and the doctrine of marriage, which are ontologically related, as the late Pope John Paul II demonstrated in his theology of the body.[18] The crisis of faith in which we find ourselves today constitutes a situation of confession (*status confessionis*). In such a situation "nothing is an indifferent matter" – *nihil est adiaphoron*. A situation in which faith and morals are up for grabs is addressed not by being indifferent to the great tradition, but by reclaiming it.

---

18. See Pope John Paul II, *Man and Woman He Created Them: A Theology of the Body*, trans. Michael Waldstein (Boston: Pauline Books and Media, 2006).

# Doing Theology in the Service of the Church

**Sarah Hinlicky Wilson**

My topic is "doing theology in service of the church." If you are not a professional theologian – and I imagine the overwhelming majority of you are not – you probably wonder what this could possibly have to do with you. Even pastors are not encouraged to think seriously of themselves as theologians. The reality, though, is that we are all theologians: maybe not self-conscious theologians, maybe not very practiced theologians, but whenever we say anything about God, we are being theologians and doing theology. The church is poorly served when theology is restricted to the designated officials, just as the church is poorly served when ministry, evangelism, or service are treated as the exclusive province of anointed experts. More to the point, God himself does not desire words about him to belong only to a handful. Perhaps you remember this wonderful story from the book of Numbers:

> Moses went out and told the people the words of the Lord. And he gathered seventy men of the elders of the people and placed them around the tent. Then the Lord came down in the cloud and spoke to him, and took some of the Spirit that was on him and put it on the seventy elders. And as soon as the Spirit rested on them, they prophesied. *But they did not continue doing it.* Now two men remained in the camp, one named Eldad, and the other named

Medad, and the Spirit rested on them. They were among those registered, but they had not gone out to the tent, and so they prophesied in the camp. And a young man ran and told Moses, "Eldad and Medad are prophesying in the camp." And Joshua the son of Nun, the assistant of Moses from his youth, said, "My lord Moses, stop them." But Moses said to him, "Are you jealous for my sake? *Would that all the Lord's people were prophets, that the Lord would put His Spirit on them!*" (Numbers 11:24–29, my italics)[1]

This lecture is therefore an invitation to all of you to become the theologians you already are. Do not argue, as Jeremiah did, "Behold, I do not know how to speak, for I am only a youth" (Jer. 1:6). Do not protest, as Moses did, "I am not eloquent … but I am slow of speech and of tongue" (Ex. 4:10). Do not flee from the task as Jonah did. Since the Day of Pentecost, God has poured out his Spirit on all flesh, just as Moses hoped for, and all his people have become prophets. All of you are called to speak words about God. Herewith I present some direction to help you in going about your task. The three approaches to theology I will discuss are experience, reading, and the fear of the Lord.

## Experience

What is man, that you make so much of him, and that you set your heart on him, visit him every morning and test him every moment? How long will you not look away from me, nor leave me alone till I swallow my spit? If I sin, what do I do to you, you watcher of mankind? Why have you made me your mark? Why have I become a burden to you? Why do you not pardon my transgression and take away my iniquity? (Job 7:17–21)

---

1. All biblical citations are from the English Standard Version.

Have you eyes of flesh? Do you see as man sees?
Are your days as the days of man, or your years as a
man's years? (Job 10:4–5)

You have granted me life and steadfast love, and
your care has preserved my spirit. Yet these things
you hid in your heart; I know that this was your
purpose. (Job 10:12–13)

Experience is probably the least likely way for any Lutheran
theologian to advocate doing theology. We are famously dis-
dainful of those who make experience an explicit part of
theological method; we know that the proper source for true
theology is Holy Scripture, as interpreted through the Creeds
and Confessions.[2]

But to reject experience out of hand is a half-truth, even
when it comes to describing Lutheran theology. The question is not *whether* we will use experience but *what kind of*
experience we will use and *how* we will use it. Consider the
example of Luther himself: when he had finally penetrated
into the mysteries of St. Paul's Epistle to the Romans, he felt
as though the heavens themselves had opened and he had

---

2. This section is very much influenced by and in substantial agreement with
Ellen T. Charry, "Experience," in *The Oxford Handbook of Systematic Theology*, eds. Iain Torrance, Kathryn Tanner, and John Webster (Oxford: Oxford University Press, 2007), 412–31. Some key passages: "[T]he recipient [of Christian Theological Experience or CTE] is prepared for the
specific experience by prior familiarity with and practice of the Christian
tradition. The recipient applies mental and emotional resources to interpret it" (419). "Experience for Christian theology can only be CTE, that
is, experiences of the God Christians talk about, shaped by interactions
with revelation, scripture, tradition, worship, and Christian thought itself" (421). "[T]hose attesting to CTE are often doing so in the service
of loving Christian self-examination" (423). "The hope of CTE is to
internalize and personalize the doctrines, practices, decrees, and ordinances
of the church" (428). "…CTE is the most destabilizing of the sources of
authority because it cannot be easily controlled. Perhaps it is important
for precisely this reason… CTE is one of Christianity's most enduring
mechanisms of self-correction" (429).

been delivered from years of bondage. There is a very tight connection here between the hard-won understanding of Scripture and the personal experience that validated the truth of the new understanding.

In addition to his own personal example, Luther offered explicit guidance on what place experience should have in theology. There is the famous remark from his 1520 commentary on Psalm 5: "Living, and even more dying and being damned, is what makes a theologian, not thinking, reading, or speculating."[3] Luther's method of Bible study was *oratio, meditatio, tentatio*, which means praying, then meditating, then finally being tempted or suffering through the work of the Scripture upon you. Bible knowledge was not something that you simply inserted into your brain and left there for safekeeping; it was an active transformation and sometimes an active torment, a decidedly experiential formation in the ways of God. Then there are Luther's strong words in the *Heidelberg Disputation* about the theology of the cross and the theology of glory. Here he warns against a corrupt use of experience: namely, identifying the favor of God with what is strongest, brightest, most beautiful, most successful. That kind of experience would inevitably lead to a rejection of Jesus Christ himself. Rather we are to recognize God's hand even in what is lowly, poor, humiliated, and downtrodden: the enslaved or exiled people of Israel, the young maiden Mary pregnant out of wedlock. Furthermore, experience is what drove Luther to recognize the necessity of allowing priests to marry – an insight, of course, that he found confirmed in Scripture. We ourselves expect that through the Christian ministry people will experience the effects of law and gospel in their own

---

3. *Luthers Werke*, Kritische Gesamtausgabe, 57 vols., eds. J. F. K. Knaake, et al. (Weimar: Böhlau, 1883ff), 163, 28–29. The Latin reads "Vivendo, immo moriendo et damnando fit theologus, non intelligendo, legendo aut speculando."

lives, being driven to repent and released for joy; and experience is why we Lutherans insist so strongly on *simul justus et peccator*, a formula not found in any direct form in the Scripture itself and hotly contested by many other Christians, but we have experienced it to be true so many times over that we find any other conception of the Christian life to be ideology, not theology.

We need to talk about experience as Christian theologians because even the best of theology is not a *substitute* for human experience. Theology is not a safe haven up on a heavenly cloud that takes us out of the pain, confusion, and struggle of earthly life. Nor is it an ideology that says how things ought to be with utter disregard for how they actually are. If we were to disregard experience altogether, we would in effect be disregarding the entire creation – God's creation. Perhaps it would be easier for those who shy away from the term "experience" to replace it with "history." We Lutherans are generally comfortable talking about God's historical involvement in the lives of his creatures. History is simply the long accumulation of human experience, from that of individuals to that of entire peoples and nations. Scripture is the record of Israel and the disciples' historical experience with God – an expansive experience that invites us to share in it. But we are not only to read in Scripture about justification by faith: we are to be justified by faith! We are not only to affirm what the Bible says about the new life in the Spirit: we are to participate in the new life in the Spirit!

Theology is not a substitute for experience, but it is a guide in the right interpretation of experience. All experience is interpreted. That's what distinguishes us from animals. Things don't simply happen to us; we try constantly to make sense out of what happens, stringing together a coherent narrative out of our lives. Left to ourselves, we would make a real mess out of our interpretations. Without the formative logic of the gospel, the rich and successful would assume they got that way out of their own particular merit; the poor and hurting would assume they did something wrong to deserve it; and the wicked would infer that no punishment awaits their evil deeds. Good theology *re*-interprets our false interpretations of our own experience according to the real norms of the gospel. It also proposes other possible experiences, counter-experiences, to balance those that the world sends our way: the experience of prayer, the experience of participation in the Lord's Supper, the experience of the mutual consolation of the Christian faithful, the experience of love and self-giving, the experience of repentance and forgiveness.

What about the other direction? Theology interprets and directs experience, but does experience interpret and direct theology? This is a difficult matter, but I think the conversation has too often been arrested by disputes over whether any particular experience can be normative. Let us assume that no experience, other than the experience recorded in Holy Scripture, is normative for everyone else; but let us then also acknowledge that each of us has to live with the experience given to us – which for us personally, anyway, *is* normative – and that we each have to make sense of our own personal experience in the light of the gospel.

To put it more directly, you are entitled to the questions and tentative conclusions that your own life experience forces upon you. A resilient theologian will take up the challenge of personal experience and demand a good answer from theology – and if theology has failed to do justice to that experience, then a theologian will press on and search and pray until a better answer is found. Sometimes theology gets so profoundly stuck in a rut that only a flood of experience can set it free again – as happened, for example, in Apartheid South Africa, where white supremacist Christian readings of the Israelite invasion of Canaan and Romans 13 finally had to give way to the counter-experience of marginalized, brutalized African Christians who were reading Exodus, the stories of corrupt Israelite kings, and the interracial unity of the Book of Acts. The same thing happened in the Reformation, when the huge dissonance between church tradition and the actual lives of Christians could no longer be sustained. Experience did not lay its claims apart from Scripture, but Scripture needed the pressure of experience to be unlocked.

The challenging interface between theology and experience is modeled in the Scripture itself, supremely in the book of Job. We are most familiar with Satan's torment of Job at the beginning and Job's vindication at the end, but the bulk of the book is Job enduring the platitudes of his theologian friends. These know-it-alls are completely convinced that Job's sufferings happen because of his own personal wickedness – and they quote generously from Deuteronomy and other parts of the Old Testament to prove it. Job's sharp responses are a much-needed warning against anyone who would glibly interpret another's experience. "You see my calamity and are afraid," he says (6:21). "In the thought of one who is at ease there is contempt for misfortune" (12:5). "Will you speak falsely for God and speak deceitfully for him? Will you show partiality toward him? Will you plead the case for God? Will it be well with you when he searches you out? Or can you deceive Him, as one deceives a man?" (13:7–9). "Your maxims are proverbs of ashes; your defenses are defenses of clay" (13:12). "Miserable comforters are you all. I also could speak as you do, if you were in my place; I could join words together against you and shake my head at you" (16:2, 4).

Job insists throughout the book that he is entitled to his questions and that he is entitled to an answer. He also realizes what little chance he has: who can argue with God and get away with it? The deck is stacked, the game is rigged. "Behold, he snatches away; who can turn him back? Who will say to him, 'What are you doing?' ... Though I am in the right, I cannot answer him; I must appeal for mercy to my accuser.... If it is a contest of strength, behold, he is mighty! If it is a matter of justice, who can summon him? Though I am in the right, my own mouth would condemn me; though I am blameless, he would prove me perverse" (9:12, 15, 19–20). This is hardly quiet, obedient piety. It's no surprise that his friends were scandalized by his bitter forthrightness.

But as we know, it was Job who was vindicated in the end, not his friends. This doesn't mean that Job was entirely *right*. There was much he didn't understand, and he confessed his own limitations in the final chapter. The difference was that it was no longer the glib theologians who were answering him but God in person – who, actually, offered no explanation whatsoever regarding his treatment of the good or the wicked. God's only self-defense is that he is the creator. But even that is balm to Job's wounds because, in his own words, "I had heard of You by the hearing of the ear, but now my eye sees You" (42:5). Nothing but the presence of God himself – nothing but the *experience* of God – can ultimately satisfy our questions and griefs. God, for his part, condemns the others: "My anger burns against you [Eliphaz] and your two friends, for you have not spoken [to] me what is right, as my servant Job has."[4] They *substituted* theology for experience, correct answers for prayerful protests, self-justification for friendship. Sometimes they had the right answers, but they had them at the expense of love for their friend Job. It's striking that the friends could not be restored to God unless Job offered a sacrifice on their behalf – but also that Job's own fortunes would not be restored until he did so. The right speech *about* God and *to* God had to lead to the reconciliation of these three estranged parties.

---

4. My translation here deviates from the ESV to read "to Me" rather than "of Me"; to see why, read Kathryn Schifferdecker, "Job's Speech about and to God," *Lutheran Forum* 45/2 (2011), 12–15.

## Reading

And all the people gathered as one man into the square before the Water Gate. And they told Ezra the scribe to bring the Book of the Law of Moses that the Lord had commanded Israel. So Ezra the priest ... read from it facing the square before the Water Gate from early morning until midday, in the presence of the men and the women and those who could understand. And the ears of all the people were attentive to the Book of the Law... And Ezra opened the book in the sight of all the people, for he was above all the people, and as he opened it all the people stood. And Ezra blessed the Lord, the great God, and all the people answered, "Amen, Amen," lifting up their hands. And they bowed their heads and worshiped the Lord with their faces to the ground... The Levites helped the people to understand the Law, while the people remained in their places. *They read from the book, from the Law of God, clearly, and they gave the sense, so that the people understood the reading.* And Nehemiah, who was the governor, and Ezra the priest and scribe, and the Levites who taught the people said to all the people, "This day is holy to the Lord your God; do not mourn or weep." For all the people wept as they heard the words of the Law. Then he said to them, "Go your way. Eat the fat and drink sweet wine and send portions to anyone who has nothing ready, for this day is holy to our Lord. And do not be grieved, for the joy of the Lord is your strength." So the Levites calmed all the people, saying, "Be quiet, for this day is holy; do not be grieved." And all the people went their way to eat and drink and to send portions and to make great rejoicing, *because they had understood the words that were declared to them.* (Nehemiah 8:1–2a, 3, 5–6, 7b–12, my italics)

Continuing from experience to reading may seem to be a blatant contradiction of Luther's rule that I mentioned a little earlier. But, of course, in typical fashion, Luther was overstating his case to make a point. As a theologian, you are not uninvolved in what you are talking about – to suppose otherwise was Job's friends' mistake. God is not some static object to be peered at under a microscope or through a telescope. But once you have recognized your deep personal involvement in theology, your *life-and-death-at-stake* involvement, then it is indeed a good and wise thing to read books. Lots of books. A broad range of books.

You need to read for two reasons. First: as long as you are pursuing the theological meaning of your own experience only – or of those in the immediate circle around you – you are going to be limited, perhaps trapped, and probably skewed in your interpretations, because of the sinful human inclination to be curved inward instead of outward. Broad reading gives you the right kind of distance on your own experience – not to put you back into the position of an unaffected observer, but to see your experience within the community of the whole church and indeed of the whole world. Such reading helps you grow from the *pro me*, the "for me," that is the starting point of reconciliation with God, to the joyful exchange, where others' experiences become your own, as St. Paul describes it: "If one member suffers, all suffer together; if one member is honored, all rejoice together" (I Cor. 12:26).

Make no mistake, it will require diligence and trust in God to seek out experiences that do not conform to your own. It will require even more to make those experiences your own; to pursue questions that are not your own for the sake of your neighbor; to internalize the truth that, if it happens to another member of the body, then it really does also happen to you. If we are truly members of the one body of Christ, then what happens to women is of enormous concern to men; what happens to rural Latinos is of enormous concern to urban Americans; what happens to the poor and enslaved is of enormous concern to the free and well-fed – and vice versa. We will never be able to experience all of these realities personally, and for most of us the range of our acquaintances will never even begin to span the breadth of human experience. But through the miraculous gift of reading, we can transcend our local and temporal limitations to discover all the places and people that God has made and wants to redeem. We can get beyond the self-justification that is the temptation of our own experience. There are certainly universals in human experience, and reading helps us identify those, too, but nobody lives inside a universal. We live inside all the millions of details of our own particular lives. An expansive and charitable vision of humanity made in God's image requires plunging into the details, not hiding behind the universals.

The other reason you need to read is for the sake of the answers you will not otherwise find. We all inherit a thought-world, trained in certain patterns of thinking and taught to ask particular kinds of questions. We assume the terms of debate that have been set in advance. For many people, the pressure to think the way society wants them to think is so great that it simply extinguishes the flame in their minds altogether. They become parrots or puppets, repeating what has already been said a thousand times before, cranking up the heat but shedding no light.

Such mindlessness is utterly contrary to the spirit of the Reformation. Luther and his friends, inspired by the humanist movement, made use of every resource they could lay their hands on – studying the ancient languages afresh, going back to the sources, experimenting in a whole range of genres from philosophy to hymnody to pastoral letters to doctrinal treatises. Luther was not simply an angry young man who objected to everything he saw out of sheer orneriness. He was a *reader* who finally realized it was necessary to reframe the entire conversation surrounding faith and salvation. Left to the limits of his own mind, he festered with anxiety and uncertainty. His personal experience was a trap, and within himself there were no resources for getting out. It was an external word – in his case, the external word of God in holy Scripture – that jolted him out of his stuck place.[5] It turned out that a lot of other people were stuck, too, and when they read how he'd been unstuck, they also were set free.

It is no accident, then, that after the gospel itself the greatest passion of the Lutheran Reformers was education. They pushed for the education of as many people as possible, financing the poor, even setting up schools for girls and employing female teachers – a truly progressive project for its time. Education has been a premier Lutheran social justice value ever since. The Reformers' efforts led to the tremendous growth of literacy in Europe. The laity's support of the Reformation stemmed from their ability to read the Bible and the rich devotional material penned for them by pastors and theologians, and the laity in turn contributed writings that flowed out of their own readings. The Lutheran tradition flourished because of its commitment to reading, and reading sustained the Lutheran tradition even after the initial fires of reform died down.

But such a commitment to careful thought and a persistent search for truth through broad reading hardly characterizes the life of our church and congregations today. We have very much absorbed the American disdain for the patience and struggle it takes to read and understand anything that is not immediately accessible – and the ramifications of such cheap thought are evident throughout our society, not only

---

5. It's worth noting that Luther tested his newfound insight against other readers' interpretations by going back to Augustine's treatise *On the Spirit and the Letter*, where, to his great relief, his own reading and experience were confirmed.

in our churches, to everyone's detriment. We are a nation that has become addicted to sensationalistic sound bites, while complex, nuanced arguments are dismissed and ignored. We are rapidly reworking ourselves into a people that can be easily manipulated and deceived. Our current state of partisan politics and culture wars is a sorry outcome for the oldest and most stable democracy on the planet.

Is it possible that we could be the leaven in this heavy lump, for the good of church and society alike? Could we not pursue guerilla warfare against over-simplification, false advertising, and mudslinging by insisting on real arguments, thoughtful questions, and humility in the face of complexity, wherever we go and to whomever we talk? Moses longed for all of God's people to be prophets; First Peter says the church is a holy nation of priests; I would like us to be deacons – of ideas. I would like us to be the curators and servants of rich ideas, intricate thoughts, finely-tuned arguments, caring for their well-being and the well-being of human minds, just as deacons care for the bodily well-being of the sick and hungry. It is a charism that would honor our heritage and serve our contemporaries at the same time.

So far I have been advocating broad reading – reading that opens us up to the whole range of human experience as well as the whole range of human analysis and answers to life's besetting questions. But now I wish to turn my attention to deep reading, which might just as well be called "re-reading" and at some point will merge into memorizing or learning "by heart," a very evocative turn of phrase – and I have in mind one book in particular, namely, the holy Bible. If there is one thing we Lutherans know about our theology, it's that it's biblical. In fact, our theology is *so* biblical that we no longer have any need to read the Bible ourselves.

Allow me to make some uncomfortable observations on the state of parish life in American Lutheranism, regarding our relationship to theological reading generally and to the holy Scripture specifically. When I look around, this is what I see. I see pastors who excuse the atrophying of their minds on the grounds of their ministerial duties; pastors who read the Scriptures only professionally for sermon-writing, not as food for their souls; pastors who abandon their explorations in all the various theological disciplines after seminary has ended. At the same time, looking at parish life, I see congregations that resent the time their pastors spend reading on the assumption that it would be better spent on other more "practical" things; congregations that abhor the idea of the pastor as a true spiritual leader who constantly grows in faith and knowledge, expecting instead an obedient religious professional hired to perform services; congregations that ignore their own mandate to be students and readers of the Scriptures, whether in relief or shame, preferring to leave such things to the experts.

I look on this and I'm embarrassed to think of the triumph of the Reformers in translating the Bible for the whole people of God, who now regard it with such indifference. I look at the amazing work still being done by Bible translators today and wonder how our hearts have grown so cold. I think of the Israelites weeping at hearing the Scripture read to them for the first time since they returned to Jerusalem after their Babylonian exile, accompanied by an army of Levites explaining it to the women and men and children, and then sending them home to have a feast and rejoice because on that holy day they had heard the Word of God and understood it. Would that all the people of God were weeping, feasting Israelites and interpreting, explaining Levites!

We have no business calling ourselves after Luther's name if we are not willing to read the book he loved best, if we have been scared off of it by fundamentalists and revisionists alike. The Scripture is the cradle of the Christ child – not the heavy stick of a wannabe theocracy, not a conspiracy that progressive postmoderns are going to liberate us from, not a dull droning blah to be repeated ritualistically without understanding. It is a treasure in earthen vessels, both human and divine, strong enough to survive our critical study, deep enough to reward our endless longings, wise enough to handle our hardest questions, strange enough to shatter our blasé boredom, shocking enough to elicit our ethical worries, and beautiful enough to give us a peek behind the temple curtain at the Holy of Holies.

If you are going to become the theologian you already are, you have to read this book. It's not enough to hear it once a week in four short, decontextualized readings; it's not enough to flip through it in the process of writing a sermon. You need to read it, you need to linger over it, you need to get out of your familiar ruts, you need to learn pieces by heart.[6] Your reading needs to grow into the mystical reading that the prophet Ezekiel describes:

---

6. My thoughts here are gratefully influenced by Paul Griffiths's *Religious Reading: The Place of Reading in the Practice of Religion* (New York: Oxford University Press, 1999), 41–42. Griffiths's book is a self-proclaimed "jeremiad" against modern, postmodern, academic, and consumerist approaches to reading, for which he is to be acclaimed and thanked. If there is any flaw in the book, it is the implicit inward-turning that must result from his account of religious reading; there is no sense of how religious reading empowers and enables an outward turn toward the world and other religions for the sake of proclaiming the gospel. One gets the sense that all religious readers will be perfectly immobile in their reading practice, thus conversion is *a priori* excluded. Nevertheless, two passages neatly express the same ideas I have been trying to communicate in this section. "[The holy text] is a treasure-house, an ocean, a mine: the deeper religious readers dig, the more ardently they fish, the more single-handedly they seek gold, the greater will be their reward. The basic metaphors here are those of discovery, uncovering, retrieval, opening up: religious readers read what is there to be read, and what is there to be read always precedes, exceeds, and in the end supersedes its readers. There can, according to these metaphors, be no final act of reading in which everything is uncovered, in which the mine of gold has yielded all its treasure or the fish pool has been emptied of fish. Reading, for religious readers, ends only with death, and perhaps not then: it is a continuous, ever-repeated act." "[R]eaders are seen as intrinsically capable of reading and

**129**

And the LORD said to me, "Son of man, eat whatever you find here. Eat this scroll, and go, speak to the house of Israel." So I opened my mouth, and he gave me this scroll to eat. And he said to me, "Son of man, feed your belly with this scroll that I give you and fill your stomach with it." Then I ate it, and it was in my mouth as sweet as honey. And he said to me, "Son of man, go to the house of Israel and speak with my words to them." (Ezek. 3:1–4)

So I say also to you: Feed your belly with this scroll! And then go speak the words of the Lord to all who will hear them!

## The Fear of the Lord

But now thus says the Lord,
He who created you, O Jacob,
   He who formed you, O Israel:
"Fear not, for I have redeemed you;
   I have called you by name, you are mine.
When you pass through the waters, I will be with you;
   and through the rivers, they shall not overwhelm you;
when you walk through fire you shall not be burned,
   and the flame shall not consume you.
For I am the LORD your God,
   the Holy One of Israel, your Savior.
I give Egypt as your ransom,
   Cush and Seba in exchange for you.

---

as morally required to read. Their capacity for retrieving the riches of the work by an act of reading is something intrinsic to them: they are essentially and necessarily readers, to the point where *homo lector* can be substituted for *homo sapiens* without loss and with considerable gain.... The work's intrinsic stability and fecundity as a resource is therefore matched by the reader's intrinsic stability and ingenuity as a discoverer or uncoverer."

Because you are precious in my eyes,
    and honored, and I love you,
I give men in return for you,
    peoples in exchange for your life.
Fear not, for I am with you;
    I will bring your offspring from the east,
    and from the west I will gather you.
I will say to the north, Give up,
    and to the south, Do not withhold;
bring my sons from afar
    and my daughters from the end of the earth,
everyone who is called by my name,
    whom I created for my glory,
    whom I formed and made." (Is. 43:1–7)

As we all know, Luther's explanation of the First Commandment reads, "We are to fear, love, and trust in God above all things." Each successive commandment's explanation begins, "We are to fear and love God so that…" And we have all invested a lot of time explaining to ourselves and others what exactly that "fear" means. It is not supposed to be a servile fear of God zapping us from on high but a respectful fear as we would show to a parent or ruler.

It was some time spent in parish ministry that led me to a different understanding of the fear of the Lord. Mine was not, shall we say, an entirely happy experience. I was rather staggered to discover how many decades people could spend coming to church and still not have the slightest clue about the gospel, how they could collectively make decisions that were in every detail contrary to the kind of witness our Lord Jesus Christ wanted us to make in the world. It was so demoralizing that in time the greatest dread I felt was when the phone rang – because it might be a parishioner! There were people I would have done almost anything to avoid talking to or worse yet listening to; and when I tried to steer things in a more gospel-friendly direction, I increasingly came to do so discreetly, even furtively, anxious not to be caught in the act of behaving like a Christian pastor. In short, I had stopped fearing God above all things. I had come to fear church council meetings above all things.

Re-reading the *Small Catechism* gave me the wake-up call I needed. When Luther tells us we are to fear God above all things, what he means is that we are not to fear anything *else* above all things. Our interpretations of the Catechism are misguided when they attempt to soften the kind of fear we have of God. The real issue is to break down, relativize, and dismantle the disproportionate fear we have toward so many other and thoroughly unworthy things. To fear God above everything else is to have astounding courage as we pursue our course through the world. We are to fear only God's judgment on us, not our enemies' *or* our friends'. There are worse things than death, worse things than disapproval, worse things than another phone call telling you that they cancelled church and are informing you about it. The *only* thing we need to fear is the Lord, and *he* is the one Who has promised to pass through the waters with us, to keep the fire from consuming us, to call us from all ends of the earth because we are precious in his eyes, and honored, and loved. Far from being servile, the fear of the Lord is invigorating.

Here too is a word needed not only in our church but even more so in our society. America runs on its fear. Fear controls our foreign policy, our domestic policy, our church cultures, our consumerism. Advertising doesn't sell with sex, it sells with fear. Our gun culture runs off fear and breeds more fear. Our national obsession with safety and security is the cancer of our fear. We are fearful about eating too much or too little or the wrong thing. We fear Muslims, immigrants, straight white males, overbearing mothers, ex-cons, blacks, even motorcyclists, for heaven's sake…! Fear goads us into passing laws that give us the right to shoot young men who have the wrong skin color and clothing on the grounds that we *feel* afraid. Fear allows our government to spy on us in secret and then blame the messenger when the word gets out. And think about the so-called "War on Terror": a revealing phrase that shows that the battle is against an emotion that lies within us! Why do we think we will win this war by sending drones against people on the other side of the world?

Don't expect me to argue with the fear. An honest look at the state of the world will quickly confirm us in our fear. It is entirely rational to be fearful, of nearly everything and nearly all the time, because all too often our fears are justified. But the fear that should limit itself to keeping us alert, watchful, and self-correcting of ourselves and our societies quickly becomes a god. Fear aspires to be all-consuming; it wants to define everything about our lives. We do not fear *the Lord* above all things, we fear *the worst*, and we worship that fear. We make sacrifices to it, we humble ourselves before it, and we beg its mercy. Fear is a cruel god because what should help us protect life ends up sapping all the life out of us. Our fear-based decisions and reactions promote death, not life.

I can't promise that fearlessness will guarantee you a pain-free, disaster-free, horror-free life. Nobody can. I can only pass on to you the message that was passed on to me. This is how St. John of Patmos put it:

> Then I turned to see the voice that was speaking to me, and on turning I saw seven golden lampstands, and in the midst of the lampstands one like a son of man, clothed with a long robe and with a golden sash around his chest. The hairs of his head were white, like white wool, like snow. His eyes were like a flame of fire, his feet were like burnished bronze, refined in a furnace, and his voice was like the roar

of many waters. In his right hand he held seven stars, from his mouth came a sharp two-edged sword, and his face was like the sun shining in full strength. When I saw him, I fell at his feet as though dead. But he laid his right hand on me, saying, "Fear not, I am the first and the last, and the living one. I died, and behold I am alive forevermore, and I have the keys of Death and Hades." (Rev. 1:12–18)

When you do theology, this is the God you are talking about. He has already died and is alive forevermore, so what do you have to fear? There's good reason the first word of the angels to human beings is always, "Fear not." We invest so much energy in protecting and preserving, circling the wagons or demanding change, driven on by the fear that the good will go away or that the good will never come, as if sin's power had never been broken and death itself were still calling the shots. But this is contrary to the very gospel we proclaim. We need not fear. "To live is Christ, and to die is gain" (Phil. 1:21).

If you would become the theologian you already are, strip off all these fears and hand them over to the everlasting Christ. Then turn toward the world that he intends to redeem. Face it with the joy and beauty and light of the gospel. If you are girded with the whole armor of God (Eph. 6), there is no need to add fear – or fear-mongering – to your arsenal. The gospel is enough.

## Conclusion: Awaiting Visitations

The narrative of Scripture is strung along a series of visitations – remarkable, unexpected, usually beautiful and sometimes terrible visitations. They are invasions into the mundane and conventional by a person and sometimes by the Person in whose image all persons are made: as when the three men visit Abraham and Sarah with news of a baby boy soon to follow; when Rebekah sees Isaac across a field and slides off her camel to find out who he is, drawn by the very sight of him; when Jacob kisses Rachel's mouth and weeps aloud for joy at finding her; when Moses stumbles across a burning bush and learns the name of God; when Samuel is awoken in the night by a voice crying his name; when Elizabeth is greeted by the mother of her Lord; when Paul and Silas bring the good news to a jailer in his jail; when Peter is thrown in the path of Cornelius the Gentile as the Spirit is poured out upon him; and all the many visitations when the Son of God took flesh and dwelt among us, from his somewhat unintentional healing of the hemorrhaging woman to his transforming request for hospitality at greedy Zaccheus's house.

It is a tragic thing that the word "grace" has come to be associated primarily with getting out of the consequences of our sins or setting aside the law. From the perspective of those hurt by the sins of others – which is all of us, even though we are also sinners ourselves – there is nothing gracious about *that*. Grace does not excuse the status quo of a fallen world any more than it legislates a better program of self- and world-improvement. Grace is never programmatic; it is always personal. It is always a person or the Person invading a dry, desert place with rain and flowers and new life. Faith is hearing about these invasions and awaiting the advent of such persons or the Person in your own life.

If you are going to become the theologian you already are, then your theology will have to emerge from your own expectation of visitations and experience of visitations. I invite you to immerse yourself in the words of those who have been visited themselves, as recorded in Scripture and elsewhere, so that when the hour comes you can welcome your own visitations without fear but with great and joyful understanding. And I exhort you to share the news of such visita-

135

tions, your own and others', with those who have not yet experienced any gracious visitations at all. Perhaps you will be called upon to be a visitation in the life of someone who is in need of one.[7] May that grace be shed upon every theologian of the church: to be a visitation of grace in the world's dry and dusty places.

7. The Russian Orthodox St. Seraphim of Sarov, after a long period of seclusion and spiritual struggle, threw open the doors of his hermitage to the world and greeted every visitor with the appellation, "My joy!" This is as good an image of a saint as any: someone who is not only a visitation to others but who welcomes everyone, "saintly" or not, as a heaven-sent visitation.

Made in the USA
Charleston, SC
20 October 2014